Counseling
and the
Demonic

RESOURCES FOR
CHRISTIAN COUNSELING

RESOURCES FOR CHRISTIAN COUNSELING

VOLUME   SEVENTEEN

Counseling and the Demonic

RODGER K. BUFFORD, Ph.D.

RESOURCES FOR CHRISTIAN COUNSELING

General Editor

Gary R. Collins, Ph.D.

WORD BOOKS
PUBLISHER
DALLAS, TEXAS

A DIVISION OF
WORD, INCORPORATED

Library of Congress Cataloging-in-Publication Data

Bufford, Rodger K.
    Counseling and the demonic.

    (Resources for Christian counseling; v. 17)
    Bibliography: p.
    Includes index.
    1. Devil. 2. Demonology.   3. Mental illness.
4. Pastoral counseling. I. Title. II. Series.
BT981.B76 1988   235'.4   88-27980
ISBN 0-8499-0599-0

Printed in the United States of America
89801239 AGF   987654321

CONTENTS

EDITOR'S PREFACE

Five centuries ago, two Dominican monks in Germany published a famous book titled *Malleus Maleficarum* (The Witch Hammer). The treatise argued for the existence of witches, described the signs by which they could be detected, and gave instructions for their elimination. Throughout Europe the book was read widely and used as justification for the torture and violent deaths of hundreds of thousands of mentally ill men, women, and children, all of whom were thought to be demon possessed. Physicians, clergy, and laypersons all assumed that psychopathology was the result of witchcraft or demonic influence. Many people would have agreed with a sixteenth-century physician named Daniel Sennert who believed that demon-infested bodies should be treated so violently that the demons would be forced to leave.

A few voices challenged this kind of thinking. In the mid-1500s, for example, Johann Weyer wrote a book to refute the *Malleus*. Weyer argued against the existence of witchcraft and demonology. Despite criticism and abuse from his colleagues, the doctor maintained that mental illness was evidence of sickness and he condemned both exorcism and the practice of torture.

At the time, Weyer was accused of being a protector of witches, but slowly his views began to prevail—perhaps in reaction to the horrible and inhumane mistreatment of so many mentally disturbed people. Treatment became more compassionate, and thinking about mental illness also changed. Belief in demons was discarded along with the torturous methods that had been prevalent for decades.

As a result, modern books on psychiatry or abnormal psychology rarely mention the demonic, except as evidence of the ignorant and superstitious thinking of a bygone prescientific era.

A few flamboyant evangelists and exorcists have always clung to sensationalist views of the demonic, but these perspectives have tended to be dismissed as evidence of scientific ignorance or fanaticism. Some more modern and better-informed believers have developed detailed theories of demonology based on their exorcism experiences and supposed conversations with demons. But such theories have not always been taken seriously because they fail to show an understanding of clinical psychopathology, they rarely have much if any scriptural basis, and they often overlook the fact that Satan and his hosts are liars (John 8:44) who can't be expected to reveal truth about themselves.

Within recent years, however, there has been increasing interest in the demonic. Even some secular writers have acknowledged that evil forces do exist, forces that are not explained by scientific knowledge.

This awareness is not news to students of the Bible. In his letter to the Ephesians, Paul warned that believers (this includes Christian counselors) are in a battle, "not against flesh and blood, but against the rulers, against the authorities, against the powers of this dark world and against the spiritual forces of evil in the heavenly realms" (Eph. 6:12 NIV). In ourselves, we are powerless to resist these forces or to stand against the "devil's schemes." But according to the Bible, the devil and his cohorts are already defeated. They can be resisted by believers who are humble men and women of prayer, standing "firm in the faith," and able to use "the sword of the Spirit, which is the word of God."

Several years ago, the Christian Medical Society sponsored a conference on the demonic for a group of evangelical physicians, counselors, and Bible scholars. About fifty of us gathered for three days at Notre Dame University where we discussed papers and considered the nature of demonism. The tone of the discussion was friendly, but often we disagreed about what was demonic and what was pathological. Some seemed to think all deviant behavior was demonic—even when there was evidence of clear physical and psychological pathology. Others appeared to be skeptical of any reference to satanic forces. The Notre Dame conference did not anticipate the heat of debate that swirls around this topic today.

When I first proposed a book on counseling and the demonic, my colleagues at Word and I agreed that such a book should not be written by an author who would explain away the demonic; but neither did we want someone who tended to see a demon behind every evidence of unusual behavior. I believe Rodger Bufford is a writer who brings an admirable balance to this debate. Trained and experienced as a professional psychologist, he is also a Bible scholar (as the following pages show) and professor of counseling in a respected evangelical seminary. At a time of confusion, excesses (even among some evangelicals), and disagreement, Dr. Bufford brings clarity and balance.

It is significant that we include a book on counseling and the demonic in a series of volumes that are intended to be practical and helpful. Written by counseling experts, each of whom has a strong Christian commitment and extensive counseling experience, the books in this series are meant to be examples of accurate psychology and careful use of Scripture. Each is intended to have a clear evangelical perspective, careful documentation, a strong practical orientation, and freedom from the sweeping statements and undocumented rhetoric that sometimes characterize writing in the counseling field. Our goal is to provide books that are clearly written, useful, up-to-date overviews of the issues faced by contemporary Christian counselors. All of the Resources for Christian Counseling books have similar

———————————————

bindings and together they are intended to comprise a helpful encyclopedia of Christian counseling.

Rodger Bufford, the author of this book, is chairman of the department of psychology and director of the doctoral program in counseling at Western Baptist Seminary in Portland, Oregon. As an author, counselor, teacher, and conference speaker, he frequently comes in contact with pastors, professional counselors, and others who have questions about the demonic. The pages that follow reflect careful thought, detailed examination of the Scriptures, a familiarity with the increasing professional literature in this field, and personal counseling experience. As an added plus, Rodger's wife Kathleen is a professional writer whose expertise has helped to make this an especially clear and well-written volume.

It is inevitable, perhaps, that a book on counseling and the demonic will be controversial. Some may disagree with the author's conclusions, but his work gives a fresh look at an old but increasingly relevant subject. This is a volume that surely will be studied carefully by counselors and others in the years to come. I am glad to have it in this series of counseling books.

Gary R. Collins, Ph.D.
Kildeer, Illinois

INTRODUCTION

If a group of Christian counselors were questioned about their experience in dealing with demonic influence, the majority probably would indicate that they have never faced anything demonic. It would be easy to conclude that the average Christian counselor is rarely faced with this problem. But such a conclusion would be a serious error.

Throughout human history the question of demonic influence has been a controversial one. It continues to be so now, when there are two widely held views. According to the first view, demons are everywhere. Those who believe this are preoccupied with demons and with efforts to appease, avoid, or escape them. The second view discounts demons, looking on them as irrelevant, at best, or even as nonexistent. Both these views are mistaken. Unfortunately, reality is both less comfortable and more complex than either outlook permits.

The idea that demons are everywhere focuses attention on dealing with the demonic, to the neglect of human evil in motives and actions. The epitome of this approach is the expression, "the devil made me do it." If we think this way, we either become passive (awaiting divine action since we are not responsible for our condition or its solution) or we actively seek to drive out the demons.

In contrast, when we discount the relevance of demons or deny their reality, we magnify the role of human agents. We fail to realize that we are involved in a spiritual struggle, and that we are opposed by powerful spiritual forces. As a result, we rely on human resources and fail to use the spiritual resources available to us through the power of God and the Holy Spirit. This view seems prevalent in Western culture at the present time.

Either view is blind or short-sighted, misconstrues the problem, and fails to employ all of the resources God provides. We must recognize that the problem has both spiritual and material (or natural) dimensions. We need to make full use of the resources which God provides, both material and spiritual.

As the following pages will show, the tendency to polarize the material and spiritual dimensions produces disagreement over whether demonic influence or mental disorders account for unusual human behavior. This disagreement has a long history, and continues both inside and outside the Christian church. It will be our goal to examine both sides of this issue, to suggest that mental disorders and demonic influence are related, and to recommend ways to identify and treat persons experiencing demonic involvement.

As we shall see, demonic influence is far more common than most of us think. Strategies for dealing with demonic influence are clearly presented in Scripture, yet they are little practiced. It is my prayer that this book will help many to more clearly identify the problem, and to practice biblical solutions.

My interest in the issue of counseling and the demonic was sparked several years ago by the questions of those with whom I counseled. As I pondered and studied the issues involved, I discovered that I often dealt with spiritual issues, and that many of the individuals with whom I counseled were at some level or other influenced by Satan and demons, although I rarely encountered people who were possessed. More and more over the years I have come to realize that in counseling I am involved in the task of "taking on the gods."[1]

This book looks directly at the question of how the Bible presents demonism, and places demonic influence in the context of the broader biblical teachings about evil in the world and the agents of evil, including Satan and fallen angels, as well as Christian and unbelieving persons. Biblical accounts of demonism and the work of Satan and his agents are compared and contrasted with the American Psychiatric Association's *Diagnostic and Statistical Manual of Mental Disorders* (DSM-III-R).[2] After defining the problem and setting it in context, biblical principles for dealing with demonism are addressed along with practical suggestions from psychology and counseling. Examples from the counseling office are given to illustrate various approaches.

Because all evil as we know it, including physical illness, mental disorders, and social aberrations, begins with the influence of Satan and is often ascribed to the will of Satan in subsequent biblical accounts, it is of primary importance that we examine the nature of this personification of evil and his manifestations in people's lives. Thus, in the first section of the book we will address biblical teaching about the demonic, beginning with the person and work of Satan and examining biblical accounts of the occult in order to draw general principles from these accounts. Then we will address the relationship of the spirit world to material existence, and draw conclusions about Satan's tactics.

In the second section of the book we will move to an examination of the defining characteristics of mental illness, compare and contrast mental illness with demonic influence, examine the implications of this analysis, and address practical strategies for helping persons who experience personal distress and crises as a result of demonic influence. We will conclude with a discussion of the tools which God has provided for Christians involved in the struggle "against the rulers, against the powers, against the world forces of this darkness, against the spiritual forces of wickedness in the heavenly places" (Eph. 6:12).

In the case studies included in this volume all names have been changed and other identifying information has been altered to protect the identity of the individuals involved. In some instances, elements from the lives of two or more individuals have been combined.

Appreciation is expressed to: Gary Collins, the series editor, for his interest in and support of this project from its inception; to Gerry Breshears and Kenneth Lloyd, who read the manuscript in its entirety and offered numerous helpful suggestions; and to Kathleen Bufford, my wife and editor, whose comments on content, organization, spelling, and myriad other details have contributed immeasurably to the readability of the final version.

The views expressed here are, ultimately, my own. It is my hope and prayer that through this book the kingdom of God will be advanced, and that help will more effectively be given those who suffer the afflictions of Satan and his demonic emissaries.

CHAPTER ONE

THE DEVIL MADE ME DO IT

Be of sober spirit, be on the alert. Your adversary, the devil, prowls about like a roaring lion, seeking someone to devour. (1 Pet. 5:8)

We live in a day in which interest in demonism and occult phenomena is growing in society at large and, as a consequence, within the Christian community as well. The following anecdotes, collected over a period of a few months as I began work on this manuscript, illustrate the practical importance of this topic, not only for the Christian public, but for the general population, the press, and the courts as well. I quote the stories as they appeared.

Church Teaching Implicated in
Drowning Death of Girl

The death of a five-year-old Seattle girl who was drowned by her mother in a Portland motel room has prompted intense criticism of a suburban Seattle Pentecostal parish which teaches that some people are possessed by demons.

Janet Cole, 37, drove from Seattle with her daughter March 20 and checked into the Ramada Inn in North Portland. There she put five-year-old Brittany into a bathtub and drowned her. Police found the girl's body on a motel bed.

Psychiatric evaluations ordered by the court described Cole as severely disturbed, and suggested that this resulted from her involvement with the Community Chapel and Bible Training Center in Burien, Washington. The $9 million complex south of Seattle started as a small fundamentalist parish, and is now run by the Rev. Donald Lee Barnett, a former Assembly of God minister.

Barnett teaches that some people, including children, can be possessed by demons, and also teaches that children who have not reached the "age of accountability" will enter heaven. Both of these teachings are common in mainstream Christianity, but court records indicated that Cole put the teachings together, and determined that she could protect her daughter from evil by killing her before she reached an age of accountability.

Reports also indicate that Cole planned to commit suicide through [a] drug overdose after killing her daughter. Cole called police about her daughter's death, according to police reports.[1]

Satan's Servant or Clever Con Man?
Britons Wonder

MAIDSTONE, England—Beneath the heavy bronze British coat-of-arms and in front of a bewigged judge in the local court, a bizarre trial focusing on the power of the devil is fascinating this nation of established Christianity.

The question is whether Derry Mainwaring Knight, a

striking 280-pound presence, is Satan's satrap, or an extraordinary con-man.

He is accused of deceiving church and society leaders out of £300,000 in what might be called a satanic sting.

If the prosecution is right, he persuaded his victims, all committed Christians, to part with their money through an anti-devil scam designed to finance his licentious high-life.

If the defense is right, he used the funds to try to promote his own ascension within the satanic cult to get into position to rob it of its power by destroying its all-important regalia, including a chalice, a sceptre, a sword and a throne.

Is it a case of good vs. evil, or human gullibility vs. criminal greed?

. . . .

"Satanism is far more rampant in this country than people believe," said Susan Sainsbury, wife of multimillionaire Tim Sainsbury, Tory member of Parliament. Sainsbury is heir to a grocery fortune.[2]

Satan Promotes Church
Satan has joined an advertising campaign for St. James Lutheran Church in Portland. The devil, probably not a willing participant in the promotion, is pictured in bus advertising for the church saying, "I don't have a prayer at 1315 S.W. Park"—the address of the church.

"I guess you could say the devil made me do it," the Rev. Joe Smith explained. "This church is interested in being open to people. Rather than beating them over the head with a steeple, we thought we'd try humor."[3]

Channeling
One of the latest forms of spiritualistic phenomena to appear in the United States is known as "channeling." While some do not believe that this form of activity involves demonic influence, others clearly believe that it does.

In California these days, consumers can consult a reincarnated "spirit" for as little as $10 or as much as $1500 an hour. Hundreds, possibly thousands, do so each week.

. . . Channel, observers point out, is a new name for medium, someone who professes to have the power to communicate with the dead . . . .

Last year, J. Z. Knight, a Yelm, Washington woman became perhaps the nation's best-known channel after the entity she says she speaks for, a 35,000-year-old man named Ramtha, was described in a best-selling book by the actress Shirley MacLaine.[4]

The phenomena included in channeling are "as simple as an artist's creative inspiration or as complicated as 'entities' speaking through a person's body (much as a television set picks up electrical energy)."[5] Channeling is a contemporary version of the spiritualism of the 1850s in which mediums and clairvoyants held seances to contact dead loved ones.

Channeling has much diversity, but a certain characteristic pattern as well. Common features include: the use of stilted phrases, foreign accents—often changing inconsistently—emphasis on the view that each person is god and needs only to look within, and the use of exotic names such as Myissa, Quax, and Ramtha. In addition, most "channelers" seem to have a background of sales and human potential training.[6] This last feature suggests that there may be a common pattern for the development of channeling phenomena.

While only illustrative, articles like these suggest that the issue of Satan and demons is a live one in our contemporary world. Although Satan has been out of fashion for most of the twentieth century, interest in the occult has revived in the last two decades.

Several industries are not only cashing in on the rise of this phenomenon, but actively promoting it as well. In the late 1960s and early 1970s movies such as *Rosemary's Baby, Poltergeist,* and *The Exorcist* came into the entertainment market; more recently, we've been offered *The Prince of Darkness.*

Popular parlor games that encourage an openness to spirit powers are the Ouija board and the use of tarot cards. Somewhat more recent, and very successful in some quarters, is the game Dungeons and Dragons, in which the players are able to take on imaginary magical powers.

The entertainment industry has also brought to contemporary Western society a number of rock groups with names, costuming, and popular songs that evoke prevailing conceptions of occultic phenomena and of Satan himself. Among them are KISS (Knights in Service to Satan), AC/DC, Judas Priest, and a number of others.

At the same time, we see an apparent increase in actual cultic and occultic rituals. I view horoscopes, published in the daily papers, as a part of these. Witches and warlocks openly acknowledge their practices, and covens may be readily found in major cities. A satanic cult has been openly started in the San Francisco area. There have been reports even of ritual slayings of animal and, apparently, human sacrifices.

While some of these phenomena are quite blatant, it seems likely that more subtle forms of influence are more effective in most instances. C. S. Lewis captures this notion very dramatically in his space trilogy, *Out of the Silent Planet, Perelandra,* and *That Hideous Strength.* In these novels, Lewis introduces the notion of being "bent." Just as a tree is shaped to the gardener's design by gradually increasing the degree of bend in its limbs, so people are shaped to Satan's purpose by being pressed ever so gradually to depart from the straight and narrow. Lewis's point is that what is dangerous to truth is not the full 180-degree bend of the blatant lie; anyone will recognize such obvious falsehood. Rather, the greatest danger comes from truth with a slight twist.[7]

As the subtlety and variety of his approaches demonstrate, Satan is a being of vast intelligence and ability. He is a wily adversary who knows where we are most vulnerable. Consequently, we can expect that his methods will be adapted for what he deems most effective in the current intellectual, philosophical, and political climate. If we are to be effective in combating him we must understand his strategy and tactics; only thus can we recognize and defend against his attacks before we are overwhelmed. In order to effectively guard against this adversary we must avoid two common contemporary errors: 1) spiritualizing all of our personal struggles as demonic, and thus neglecting the affect of the world and the flesh, or 2) materializing our personal struggles so that we acknowledge the world and the flesh, but ignore or even deny the reality of the devil.

As interest in occult and demonic phenomena is increasing, many within the church have become involved in some of these activities, believing they are "innocent recreation."

> If the current publicity is a valid indication that more demonic activity is occurring, then Christians should be aware that renewed spiritual warfare is at hand. The Scriptures command believers to be aware of the devil's activities and schemes (2 Cor. 2:11). Once aware of Satan's battle plans they are to put on God's armor (Eph. 6:11–20), and resist Satan's attacks (James 4:7).[8]

In a recent article, Billy Graham told the Southern Baptist Convention that the "scandals involving television preachers were the work of the devil." Apparently referring to the scandal involving Jim and Tammy Bakker and PTL, Graham said: "When I started out, we had to contend with the image of Elmer Gantry. And we had lived down that image until it's been resurrected by the devil."[9]

If as believers we choose to take seriously the reality of demons and of spiritual warfare, then we must understand the nature and scope of demonic activity and be prepared to respond according to biblical guidelines in dealing with this challenge. The purpose of this book is to help counselors better understand the nature of spiritual warfare and their roles as agents in this cosmic conflict, particularly in the context of counseling.

It is natural that among pastors, psychologists, and others concerned with the care and growth of Christians, questions should arise regarding how to deal with demonism within the church. Answers to these questions are diverse, though those who are most vocal about these issues often represent one of two extreme views. One view focuses on exorcisms and the casting out of demons, even from believers. The other, to a greater or lesser degree, makes light of the possibility that Christians may come under demonic influence. Any thoroughgoing effort to develop a comprehensive approach to counseling and psychotherapy from a Christian perspective must address all aspects of these issues.

CHAPTER TWO

SATAN IS ALIVE AND ACTIVE

Demons are satanic emissaries. If we are to consider meaningfully the activities of demons, and techniques for dealing with their influence, we must first consider the existence and character of their chief—"the prince of the power of the air," "the ruler of this world."

Michael Green proposes seven lines of evidence in support of belief in Satan.[1] The first is philosophical. It is absurd to imagine a universe of rational intellect without a supreme Reason, God. Similarly, it is most reasonable to suppose an organizing spirit of supreme evil behind all that is corrupt and malign. Second, theology teaches us to believe in a creator-God who, though unseen, is personal and good, and is concerned with redeeming persons from the evil into which they have fallen. Such evil requires a devil, a personal force of evil, unless we are to posit a merciless, tyrannical God.

Third, the world around us is full of destructive forces; most notable among these is the human capacity and choice to marshal natural forces toward evil ends. Fourth is the fact of temptation, exposure to all manner of delightful inducements to do wrong. The universality of such experience suggests some organizing principle behind them. Fifth, there are many who actively worship Satan; these have often discovered remarkable powers, both real and terrible. Sixth, throughout Scripture we find explicit and detailed teachings about Satan, particularly in the Gospels. Finally, Christ himself clearly believed in Satan and engaged in conflict with him. This conflict led to the cross —and to the further battle which continues today.[2]

In summarizing his discussion of the person of Satan, Dickason notes that Satan is a creature made by God, a spirit being as other angels, of the class of cherubim, and probably appointed to the highest rank among all creatures, second only to God. This lofty position, however, was not enough to satisfy him. He sought to usurp the position of God himself.[3] While Dickason's view of Satan's former rank is controversial, it seems clear that Satan is "an organizing intellect, a single focus and fount of evil inspiration, . . . a power of concentrated and hateful wickedness."[4]

In the material which follows we will examine the names of Satan, his character, his activities, the forces which he leads, his relationship to the believer, and his basic plan. The majority of this material will be drawn from Scripture.

NAMES OF SATAN

Names, as they are used in Scripture, portray the character of the person. If we are to understand who Satan is, the first step is to examine his names and descriptive titles: Satan, the devil, the dragon, the serpent, Beelzebul, Belial, Lucifer, Abaddon, Appolyon, the evil one, the tempter, the god of this age, the prince of the power of the air, the ruler of this world, the prince of demons, the accuser, the deceiver, "the spirit that now works in the sons of disobedience."[5]

Satan suggests the notion of "adversary"; it comes from a Greek root which means to lie in wait or to oppose. The Hebrew word from which the word *Satan* is derived means an adversary or an enemy; however, when used with a definite article (*the* adversary), it becomes a proper name, denoting Satan.

In the New Testament we find that the devil and Satan are the same personage.[6] Satan is presented as the adversary of both God and man. His methods sometimes include direct frontal attack; however, he is also a guerrilla fighter who has mastered the techniques of sniping, bombing, and hostage-taking.

Although the Old Testament introduces Satan and clearly conveys his evil character, it is in the New Testament that we find most references to him and gain something like a full picture of his corruptness. Of the sixty-six references to Satan in the New Testament, thirty-three refer to him by this personal name, generally using the definite article, *the* Satan. An additional thirty-three references refer to him as the devil.[7]

Devil occurs only in the New Testament and is used in connection with descriptions of Satan as a traducer, a false accuser and slanderer. He slanders man before God, and God before man. His goal is to discredit each before the other.

Dragon seems to refer to a sea monster or sea serpent. In Scripture the dragon is used as a personification of both Satan and Pharaoh. The linking of Satan with a sea animal suggests that Satan may be active in the seas of the world as well as on land and in the atmosphere above the land. The dragon is portrayed as a creature of great wrath against God, and seeks to totally destroy God's people.

Serpent Reference to the serpent first occurs in the account of the events in the Garden of Eden. This name suggests that Satan is deceitful and crooked; we might say that he speaks with a forked tongue. The serpent is also identified with Satan in the New Testament (2 Cor. 11:3, 13–15).

Beelzebub (Beelzebul) The precise meaning of this name is not agreed upon. It may suggest "lord of dung" or "lord of the house." Its use is limited to the accounts in the Gospels in which the Pharisees charge that Jesus "casts out demons only by Beelzebul, the ruler of the demons" (Matt. 12:24), and to one recorded instance in which Jesus used this name (Matt. 10:25).

Belial (Beliar) Found only in the Old Testament, except for one mention in 2 Corinthians 6:15, this word is used to connote "worthlessness." The expression "sons of Belial" marks certain people as worthless persons. This is, perhaps, an understatement since it ignores Satan's capacity for active harm.

Lucifer Whether this name refers to Satan is a matter of controversy.[8] Used in reference to the morning star, this term is thought to refer to the planet Venus. Lucifer means light bearer. In the New Testament, Lucifer and Satan are one, and Satan is said to disguise himself as an angel of light (2 Cor. 11:14). Thus, Satan's character as a deceiver may also be implied by this name. However, the primary significance of the title *Lucifer* is that it draws our attention to Satan's once lofty and honored position. A similar Old Testament reference to Satan describes him as the "anointed cherub who covers" (Ezek. 28:14). How far he has fallen.

Abaddon and Appolyon These names, which occur in Revelation, characterize Satan as the destroyer, and the accuser of the brethren. In the context of Revelation we see Satan as a destroyer of the earth, and especially of mankind; however, the balance of Scripture focuses our attention on his activities as the destroyer of spiritual life.

The evil one is an expression that presents Satan as a person who personifies evil. Not only is Satan himself bent on evil, wickedness, cruelty, tyranny, violence, and the like; it is also a feature of his character that he encourages others in this direction and desires evil ends for as many as possible.

The tempter This expression captures Satan's involvement in encouraging evil in others. It is within his character to see that we notice opportunities to do wrong—the unguarded wallet . . . the attractive young man or woman who just happens to be married to another . . . the extra piece of pie when we've had enough. . . . Such temptation is not usually blatant; it is subtle, lurking just beyond our current tolerance for evil, always enticing us onward to another level of corruption.

The god of this age indicates that, whether we recognize it or not, it is Satan who stands at the head of false religion. He has his bishops and priests, his worshipers, his sacrifices, his temples. It is doubtless he who stands behind all false cults and religions which through the ages have opposed true worship. He is *The Lord of the Flies,* in William Golding's term. The world is, to a substantial degree, his domain.

The prince of the power of the air is an expression that is subject to various interpretations. Some believe it implies that Satan is the ruler in the spirit world, that he has a vast host of servants at his beck and call to carry out his desires, and that he rules over these with despotic and near-absolute power.

The ruler of this world suggests that Satan's realm of influence extends over the whole earth. In addition to ruling over his servants in the spirit world, Satan also is the power behind the throne in all forms of corrupt government. It seems significant that Jesus did not dispute Satan's claim to some sort of right of dominion on planet Earth (Matt. 4:8, 9). Other phrases which refer to Satan include "the deceiver of the whole world," "an enemy," the father of lies," "the ancient serpent," "liar," and "murderer."

Satan is a personal being, the enemy of God and man. His activity includes slander and accusation, thus implying or bringing guilt and alienation. Although he is crooked and deceitful, he has the capability of appearing as an angel of light, a minister of truth and righteousness. He is characterized by worthlessness and evil, and he encourages and promotes evil among men. He has tremendous influence over the earth, sea, and sky and is a power behind earthly kingdoms. Although not omnipresent, he has a vast host of followers who do his bidding, thus effectively extending his influence throughout the world. He is a false god, the head of false religions in their many forms and manifestations. Satan's power is so vast that even Michael, the archangel, did not dare to pronounce judgment on him, instead saying "the Lord rebuke you" (Jude 9).

THE CHARACTER OF SATAN

In addition to the names and descriptions we have already seen, many additional characteristics of Satan are presented in Scripture. Satan is a personal agent, characterized by will and knowledge. He is described as active within the sphere of this world and he is also able to enter into the presence of God.

Thus we see that Satan, once a creature of great beauty and lofty position in the service of God, is now cast down. His basic character includes murder, deception, and enmity toward God and all who would serve God. In this capacity he accuses believers constantly before God, encourages their yielding to temptation, fosters the guilty conscience, and, in all other ways he is able, he seeks to destroy and incapacitate those who would serve God. Although his ultimate doom has been pronounced, and a major victory over him was accomplished in Christ's death and resurrection, he continues to be active and powerful in the present age. Ultimately, he is to be judged, condemned, and cast into the lake of fire forever.[9]

THE ACTIVITIES OF SATAN

Some of the activities of Satan are intimated in his names and character. Satan is a tempter and seducer who encourages our every evil inclination. He exploits human weaknesses and limitations, enticing persons to sin. In doing so he uses all of the allurements of the world. He commonly tempts people to evil by the lie that they can attain a desired good through wrongdoing. In the process he deceives them by subtly questioning or denying the truth of God's revelation. We can see these activities in his approach to Eve in the Garden of Eden and again in the temptations of Jesus (Gen. 3:1–5; Matt. 4:1–11).

Satan is a counterfeiter, able to work supernatural wonders at times, such as during the testing of Pharaoh in the plagues of Egypt, thus simulating the activity of God (Exod. 7–9). He also produces false believers within the church who cannot readily be distinguished from those who belong to the kingdom of God (see Matt. 13:24–30, 37–43).

Another objective of Satan's activity is to produce spiritual blindness so that persons reject the gospel and believe in a lie, giving heed to "deceitful spirits and doctrines of demons" (1 Tim. 4:1). Satan is an accuser; he is able to enter into God's presence (Job 1) and there accuse believers of sin (Rev. 12:10). Moreover, he is very effective at reminding us of our transgressions even after they have been confessed and for-given. In this fashion he fosters crippling guilt feelings.

Although at times an accuser who induces guilt in people, Satan also is a justifier, excuser, and rationalizer who encourages others to overlook or explain away even major transgressions such as child abuse and genocide (Rom. 1:28–32).

Satan fiercely and implacably opposes God and all who would enter into his kingdom. He is pictured as snatching away the Word of God from the unsaved who might believe it (Matt. 13:19). He hinders the work and welfare of the saints (1 Thess. 2:18); if all else fails he attacks and persecutes them (1 Pet. 5:8).

Finally, with the cooperation of the person involved, usually through some form of sin, Satan can enter into a person and gain control over him or her to a remarkable degree. It is this phe-nomenon which is referred to as "possession."[10]

Although Satan is a powerful and determined adversary, it is clear that his capabilities are not without limit. He is described as a created being. God sets limits on the activities of Satan. Thus, Satan was able to afflict Job only within the boundaries set by God (Job 1:6–12; 2:1–6). He is similarly limited in his ability to harm other believers (1 Cor. 10:13). In fact, at times God uses Satan as his agent to chasten and correct erring believ-ers (1 Cor. 5:1–5).

Believers are promised that God is greater than Satan, and that nothing can separate them from God's love. God's ultimate victory over Satan is assured in the death and resurrection of Christ (Rom. 8:37–39).

Satan uses Scripture, albeit to his own deceitful ends. He quoted from the Old Testament to Jesus in the desert, seeking to provoke Jesus to disobey God the Father (Matt. 4:1–11).

In addition to being a liar and the father of lies, Satan sends out false prophets and teachers who will lead astray, if they are able, even the very elect (2 Cor. 11:13–15; see also 2 Kings 10:18–23; Jer. 2:8; 5:30–31; 14:13–16; 23:1–32ff; Matt. 7:15–16; 24:11, 24; 2 Tim. 4:3–4; 2 Pet. 2:1–3ff; 1 John 4:1; Rev. 2:20; 16:13). Satan is also able to perform miracles (see Exod. 7:11ff; Matt. 24:24; Rev. 13:11ff; cp. Rev. 16:13–14; 19:20).

At the present time, Satan's powers and activities on earth are held in check by the "Restrainer," presumably the Holy Spirit. During the end times this restraint will be temporarily removed, and there will be a tremendous outpouring of evil and many supernatural events (see, for example, Rev. 9:13–21).

Satan is not divine; he is neither omnipotent, omniscient, nor omnipresent. He has vast power, but that power is definitely limited. He is not omniscient, as is evident from his blunders during the course of history, as seen, for example, in his futile efforts to destroy the child Jesus. Satan is not omnipresent but makes his power felt world-wide through the operations of his many minions. Satan acknowledged his limitations in his conversation with Jehovah concerning Job.[11]

Satan's decision to seek to usurp the throne of God inaugurated an unrelenting cosmic struggle between Satan and God, between evil and good. By his seduction of Adam and Eve, Satan gained dominion over mankind. This dominion has been broken through the death and resurrection of Christ, but the full results of the victory won at Calvary are yet to be manifested.

The biblical picture of Satan is not dualistic. Good and evil are not presented as co-eternal principles. While Satan is seen as a mighty evil being, his kingdom is viewed as having a definite beginning and will have a definite end. The operation of evil is always viewed as being under the sovereign permission of the eternal God. God allows Satan to continue his work in order to give a cosmic demonstration of the bankruptcy of the satanic lie.[12]

THE FORCES OF WICKEDNESS

As we have noted, Satan is not omniscient, omnipresent or omnipowerful. However, he has help. When Satan chose to rebel against God he did not do so alone. Evidently a great number of angelic beings participated in the effort along with him. When Satan encountered initial defeat and was cast out of heaven, these angels accompanied him (Matt. 25:41; Rom. 8:38; 2 Pet. 2:4; Jude 6–7; Rev. 12:7–12).

Although references to demons occur a few times in the Old Testament, these are in poetic passages and they seem to be used metaphorically to refer to qualities associated with pagan deities. An evil spirit is described in the Old Testament, but is later identified with Satan.

The Old Testament is consistent in its adherence to a monistic emphasis on one God. Thus earthly (some would say natural) disasters and disease are consistently attributed to the activity of God. However, there is also a consistent emphasis on disease as a normal physical process to be dealt with largely by physical means.

[Ironically, during the intertestamental period,] so pervasive had Near Eastern superstitions become that Jews and Gentiles alike regarded the onset of disease as the work of demonic powers. In Israel, in particular, the physician was of comparatively low repute, since God was regarded as the dispenser of sickness and health alike. When superstitious beliefs in demons arose, the best the physician could do was to treat the patient by means of charms, incantations, and the like, which was a far cry from the nonmagical, empirical therapy of the Mosaic law.[13]

While not a matter of universal agreement, it appears that the best view is that devils or demons are fallen angels, and are identical with those who sided with Satan in the initial cosmic struggle between evil and good. As his agents, demons are under Satan's rule and control, they exercise his bidding and extend his influence far and wide over our world.

In addition to Satan and his fallen angels, the demons, it is clear from Scripture that all mankind outside of a personal relationship with God is also under Satan's dominion and is servant (or slave) to his ends (John 8:39–45; 1 Cor. 10:20). Thus, in the affairs of men, Satan is often the unseen "power behind the throne," the true spiritual leader and guiding force who shapes and directs the lives of men to serve his ends (2 Cor. 4:3–4; Eph. 6:12).

SATAN AND THE BELIEVER

In light of Calvary, believers are promised victory over Satan and assured that soon God will crush Satan under our feet (Gen. 3:15; 1 Cor. 15:55–57; Rev. 12:1–10; 20:1–5). As believers, we are instructed: "Resist the devil . . . and he will flee from you" (James 4:7). We are to be sober and watchful, to give the devil's schemes no opportunity for success either through carelessness or personal sinfulness (Eph. 4:26–27). The metaphors of stalking prey and of battle are used to communicate the seriousness of this matter. To succeed, the believer is instructed to "take up the whole armor of God"—truth, righteousness, the gospel of peace, faith, salvation, the Word of God, and prayer (Eph. 6:10– 20).

Other key factors in successfully resisting Satan include "the blood of the Lamb and . . . the word of their testimony, and not [loving] their life even to death" (Rev. 12:11).

SATAN'S PLAN: IDOLATRY

The original plan of Satan was to usurp the very throne of God, thus supplanting God himself (see Isa. 14:12-14). When Satan's efforts were thwarted and he was thrown down upon the earth, his activities toward this end did not cease. One aspect of Satan's current activity involves the encouragement of idolatry (Matt. 4:8–9; 1 Cor. 10:19–21).

Idolatry involves worshiping something other than the true God in some manner other than the true way. Anything which takes precedence over the true God in our thoughts and actions is idolatry. Although most people seem unaware that they practice idolatry, and many seem to believe that idolatry is rare in our contemporary societies, it is, in fact, quite common and widespread.

Any false god, idea, philosophy, habit, occupation—anything which has our primary concern and loyalty or occupies first place in our thoughts and actions, thus supplanting concern and loyalty to the true God—is idolatry. Some people keep their idols parked in their garages; others take them to the health club to keep them in shape; still others devote long hours in offices and factories, or in sporting arenas to attain their idols.

Movie, television, and rock stars are often referred to as "idols," as are sports heroes. And idols they often are. Consider, for example, the continuing cult of followers of Elvis Presley, who has now been dead for several years. Cars, boats, children, clothes, position, degrees, wives (or husbands), athletic prowess, shapely ("heavenly") bodies, desires (appetites) for food, drink, drugs, leisure, comfort or happiness, and virtually anything else we value, has the potential of becoming an idol (Phil. 3:19). Even other people can become, and often are, our idols.[14]

Job shows an understanding of the significance of idolatry when he says:

> If I have put my confidence in gold, and called fine gold
>   my trust,
> If I have gloated because my wealth was great, and
>   because my hand had secured so much;
> If I have looked at the sun when it shone, or the moon
>   going in splendor,
> And my heart became secretly enticed, and my hand
>   threw a kiss from my mouth,
> That too would have been an iniquity calling for
>   judgment,
> For I would have denied God above.   (Job 31:24–28)

The breadth of idolatry is identified by a number of Scriptures. Most persons recognize that the worship of carved images of people, or of animals, or of other living creatures is forbidden by God as idolatry (see Exod. 20:4–6; Deut. 4:14–18, 23–25; Rom. 1:24–26). Worship of heavenly objects is forbidden in the same context (Deut. 4:19).

Covetousness is explicitly referred to as idolatry (Eph. 5:5). A person's appetite for food, drink, sexual pleasures, and for recognition by others, also has the potential of becoming a false god (see Rom. 16:17–18; 1 Cor. 6:13–20; Phil. 3:18–19). Finally, the worship of demons and angels is also forbidden, and is considered idolatry.

In summing up his discussion of the issues regarding eating

meat sacrificed to idols, Paul concludes that those who sacrifice to idols unwittingly sacrifice to demons:

> What do I mean then? That a thing sacrificed to idols is anything, or that an idol is anything? No, but I say that the things which the Gentiles sacrifice, they sacrifice to demons, and not to God; and I do not want you to become sharers in demons. (1 Cor. 10:19–20)

Through this, idol worshipers are ultimately involved in worship of their head, Satan himself. At first, this suggestion may seem surprising. However, Jesus told the Pharisees "You are of your father the devil, and you want to do the desires of your father" (John 8:44). Whether they recognized it or not, in choosing not to truly serve God the Pharisees were in fact choosing to be servants of Satan. Such is true of all false worship. We will elaborate on this theme further in a later chapter.

Because "the earth is the Lord's, and all it contains" (Ps. 24:1), the good things which God has provided are to be enjoyed within the framework of his divine decrees. Even these good things, when taken outside of God's expressed will, are sinful and idolatrous.

Given the widespread practice of putting other things before God in our contemporary culture, and the reality that sacrifice to idols is essentially the same as worshiping demons, it appears that the issue in our culture is not so much whether the demonic is present as in what form it is manifested.

Most of us tend to think that our contemporary culture is far more sophisticated than that depicted in the Old Testament and that we do not have idolatry as portrayed there. Careful reflection, however, suggests some uncomfortable parallels. For example, the Israelites sacrificed their children by causing them to "pass through the fire for Molech" (2 Kings 23:10; Jer. 32:35), though this practice was clearly prohibited, and was a capital offense.[15] While little is known about Molech, it seems likely that this practice was intended to ensure good crops, and hence prosperity. Is this so different from our contemporary practice of abortion, which serves economic and social convenience through avoiding the responsibilities, costs, publicity, and time demands of unwanted children?

Other practices of worship involved the portrayal of exaggerated sexual organs. Is this so different from the *Playboy* and *Hustler* magazines, "adult" movies, and topless bars in our cities, and the preoccupation with sexual pleasures?

While superficially different, it seems likely that these activities have several common features. First, they involve seeking good things, which have been created by God to be enjoyed within divinely appointed limits, but obtaining them at times or in ways which are outside God's sovereign provision.

Second, they take precedence over God in our lives, in terms of our time commitments, money, and emotional allegiance. Third, they have behind each of them the power of Satan and his minions. As we have seen, all false worship ultimately involves worship of demons; it is choosing sides with Satan rather than with God.

Again we are faced with an illustration of the craftiness of Satan, the master deceiver. He has truly blinded the minds of our generation. Sadly, many believers are also at least partially blinded to Satan's tactics. The very fact that many doubt the presence and activity of Satan and his demons is evidence of the effectiveness of his deceptions.

SUMMARY

In this chapter we have reviewed the names, character, and activities of Satan as he relates to his minions, the fallen angels, to fallen men, and to the believer. We have seen that Satan is not merely a force or principle, but a personal agent, a usurper who sought to seize the throne of God. We saw that he is an enemy or adversary both to God and to mankind, and that he is a thoroughgoing deceiver who uses any means at his disposal to accomplish his ends of encouraging humans to join him in rebellion against God.

Satan is a being of great knowledge and power, who is the god of this age. He has at his disposal a great array of fallen angels who joined with him in his insurrection. One of Satan's chief modes of action involves fostering and encouraging all forms of false worship or idolatry, characterized centrally by giving to some aspect of creation, chiefly Satan himself, the honor, re-spect, and obedience due to God. Like the Pharisees of Jesus' day, most persons today would doubtless be astounded to be told that they belong to Satan; yet that is essentially what the Scriptures teach us. Satan has been so effective that most of us are not even aware of his active involvement in the process of fostering un-Christian worldviews and the worship of "things," of the creation of God, rather than the God of creation.

In the next chapter we will turn our focus to the activities of Satan's chief emissaries, the fallen angels or demons.

CHAPTER THREE

BIBLICAL ACCOUNTS OF SATANIC ACTIVITY

This chapter will begin with accounts of overt demonic influence and possession in the Old and New Testaments, examining the characteristic symptoms and surrounding circumstances. We will then consider biblical narratives of demonic activities which differ from the classic notions of "influence" or "possession" and conclude with a brief summary of the forms and effects of demon possession.

DEMONIC INFLUENCE AND POSSESSION

The Bible includes a number of accounts of demonic influence and possession. With but two exceptions, all of these are recorded in the Gospels. The exceptions are the account of King

Saul (1 Samuel 16) and that of the fortune-telling slave girl of Philippi (Acts 16). We will examine first the Old Testament account of Saul; then we will turn to the New Testament.

Before examining the biblical records, a cautionary note must be sounded. While there are numerous reports of demonic activity in the Bible, taken as a whole the accounts leave much unsaid. This limits our discussion. Many questions will remain unresolved. Even on issues where conclusions are drawn, often they are fraught with difficulties and it may be necessary to keep these tentative. As Oesterly notes,

> Upon a subject that bristles with so many difficulties nobody would wish to dogmatize; no conclusion that has been reached is free from serious objections, and the same is the case with that here offered . . . .[1]

The expression "demon possession" does not occur in the Old Testament. It apparently originated with Josephus, and has since been widely adopted.[2] The expression derives from several Greek verb forms used in the New Testament meaning to be under the power of a demon, to be possessed, having demons, having the spirit of an unclean demon, in the power of an unclean spirit, or troubled with unclean spirits.[3] Similarly, the Greek word "spirits" (*pneumata*) is used with a number of adjectives that indicate that the spirits are unclean, evil, more evil, deaf, dumb, or mute. There are also spirits of infirmity and divination.[4]

Old Testament

In the Old Testament literature there is no specific term that is equivalent to "demon." Supernatural phenomena are indicated by referring to "gods" (*elohim*). Thus, a devout person is referred to as a man of god. Prophetic activities are associated with the Spirit of God coming upon a person, for example, Balaam, in Numbers 24:2, or Saul, in 1 Samuel 10:10–11. Similarly, Saul's demonic affliction is reported by saying that an evil spirit of God came to Saul (1 Sam. 16:15–16, 23).

Saul The appointment of Saul as king was in response to the demands of the people of Israel to have a king rule over them "like all the nations." In discussing this matter with Samuel, God indicated that the people "have rejected me from being king over them" (1 Sam. 8:6–9). Consequently, Saul was chosen by God to be the first human king of Israel.

Soon, however, Saul disobeyed God. God instructed him to ". . . strike Amalek and utterly destroy all that he has, and do not spare him; but put to death both man and woman, child and infant, ox and sheep, camel and donkey" (1 Sam. 15:3). Instead, Saul spared the king of Amalek and the choicest of the spoils. As a result, "the Spirit of the Lord departed from Saul, and an evil spirit from the Lord terrorized him" (1 Sam. 16:14).

The spirit that afflicted Saul deserves comment. Harrison notes:

> The English versions wrongly ascribed the provenance of the phenomenon to God. In actual fact, the use of the generic term for "god" was merely intended by the author to describe the evil spirit as "powerful" or "mighty" without any inherent demonism being conveyed.[5]

Saul became possessed by a powerful evil spirit as a direct result of his own sinful conduct. The affliction of Saul by the evil spirit may have become possible in part because the Spirit of the Lord had departed from Saul. At a deeper level, however, it should be acknowledged that God, in his sovereignty, allowed this event to occur, much as God allowed Satan to afflict Job or as "the Lord hardened Pharaoh's heart" (Exod. 10:20, 27).

Some might contend that Saul was not possessed by an evil spirit or demon, arguing that he was instead mentally deranged. I believe that the biblical text supports the conclusion of demonic influence; however, even the derangement view is compatible with the conclusions which follow in later chapters.

Old Testament References Some additional references to the popular demonology of the pagan nations surrounding Israel occur in the Old Testament. For example, the term "hairy ones" or "satyrs" occurs in Leviticus 17:7, and there are references to foreign gods with no apparent demonic implications. Similarly, several Old Testament passages contain references to demons by names or titles common to ancient Near Eastern literature. The fact that all of these occur in poetic passages suggests that they are used as literary figures of speech rather than literal references.

The cosmic struggle between good and evil, represented by Satan as an implacable adversary constantly opposed to the outworking of the divine will, is not very prominent in Old Testament writings. But it is present in seed form in the account of the Fall:

And I will put enmity
Between you and the woman,
And between your seed and her seed,
He shall bruise you on the head,
And you shall bruise him on the heel.   (Gen. 3:15)

This statement looks forward prophetically to the agony and triumph of the crucifixion and resurrection.

Another principle revealed in the Old Testament is that Satan's power and influence is limited by the hand of God. We see this especially in the account of Job where God gives Satan permission to do as he wishes to Job, yet God sets a limit on the scope of Satan's action (see Job 1:12; 2:6).

New Testament Gospels

Although in classical Greek literature demons could be either good or evil, in the New Testament devils or demons are consistently presented as beings hostile to God and men. The prince of these beings is presented as Beelzebul (Beelzebub), and demons are generally regarded as his agents in the affairs of men. At a few points in the New Testament the common Greek root is used to refer to pagan deities, as when Paul gave instruction not to eat meat sacrificed to idols (i.e., demons). Otherwise, there is little reference to demons or demonism except in the Gospels. Thus the main teachings about demonism and demon possession are in the Gospel accounts of the life of Jesus Christ.

In these accounts one gets the impression that the incarnate presence of God in the person of Jesus Christ provoked an unprecedented outpouring of demonic activity in opposition to his work on earth. It seems that where the power of God is most manifest, the powers of darkness are equally apparent. Thus ". . . the evangelists depict Christ in continual conflict with evil forces."[6]

Five occurrences of demon possession are described in detail in the Gospels: the demoniac in the synagogue at Capernaum, the Gadarene demoniac, the dumb man, the daughter of the Syrophoenician woman, and the demon-possessed boy. We will examine each of these accounts in turn.

The Demoniac in the Synagogue at Capernaum As Jesus was teaching in the synagogue, this man cried out: "'What do we have to do with You, Jesus of Nazareth? Have You come to destroy us? I know who You are—the Holy One of God!'" (Mark 1:24).

In this outburst the demon demonstrated supernatural knowledge, showing a recognition of who Jesus was, and also suggesting a knowledge of God's ultimate triumph over Satan and his emissaries with the question about whether Christ had come to destroy "us." At Jesus' command to the unclean spirit to be quiet and to come out of the man, the demon cast the man down and left him.

Here we observe two features about demons. First, they have supernatural knowledge, evidently knowing both the identity of Jesus and something of God's plan for ultimate triumph over Satan and his angels. Second, we observe the power of the demon to control the demoniac physically in its ability to throw him to the ground in the process of departing at Christ's command.

The Gadarene Demoniac When the demoniac of the country of the Gadarenes met Jesus, he cried out, "'What do we have to do with You, Son of God? Have You come here to torment us before the time?'"(Matt. 8:29). Here again we observe that the demons seem to have supernatural knowledge, not only recognizing Jesus, but also anticipating that he will ultimately punish them. In addition, we note that the demoniac was so strong and violent that he was able to tear apart chains and break shackles, and could not be successfully restrained. The demoniac also continually cried aloud and gashed himself with stones.

As Jesus was casting out the demons they begged, through the demoniac, that Jesus not send them out of the country, entreating him instead to send them into a herd of pigs which was feeding nearby. Jesus agreed to do this, and the pigs promptly ran down a bank into the nearby Sea of Galilee and were drowned. This curious sequence of events suggests that demons prefer association with persons, and resist banishment from them. Even possessing the body of a pig seems preferable to being without a physical body.

Finding the demoniac "sitting down, clothed and in his right mind" (Mark 5:15) and learning what had transpired, the countrymen became frightened. While they evidently feared the demoniac, and had tried repeatedly without success to restrain him with bonds and fetters, it seems that they found the power of the One who could control the demoniac even more frightening. Thus, they begged Jesus to leave their country.

The Dumb Man In Luke's account this demoniac is described as dumb; in Matthew he is described as both blind and dumb. The accounts agree that when the demon was cast out the dumb man was able to speak (Matt. 12:22–30; Luke 11:14–26).

The casting out of this demon presented the occasion for an interchange between Jesus and the Pharisees. The Pharisees charged that Jesus "'casts out demons by Beelzebul, the ruler of the demons'" (Luke 11:15). In his reply, Jesus notes that if this were so, then Satan would be fighting against himself, thus thwarting his own purposes. In addition, Jesus notes that the sons of the Pharisees also cast out demons. Seemingly in direct contradiction to the view of the Pharisees, Jesus suggests that if he casts out demons by the "finger of God" then the kingdom of God is come.

Jesus goes on to note that when a demon is cast out it wanders through waterless places seeking rest, unable to find any. Consequently, it will seek to reenter the place from which it has been expelled.

> And when it comes, it finds it swept and put in order. Then it goes and takes along seven other spirits more evil than itself, and they go in and live there; and the last state of that man becomes worse than the first. (Luke 11:25–26)

Apparently the abode of demons, when they are cast out, is an unpleasant place; thus demons seek persons to inhabit. Also, when a demon is expelled something else must take its place or it will return. We will address this fact later.

The Daughter of the Syrophoenician Woman In this account it is unclear whether the demonically possessed daughter is even present. All we learn is that the girl is "cruelly demon-possessed" by an "unclean spirit." There is little information which we can gain about the activities of demons from this account (see Matthew 15:22–28 and Mark 7:25–30).

The Demon-Possessed Boy This child is described as epileptic and very ill; it is reported that under the influence of the demon the boy would fall into the fire and also into the water, apparently in an effort by the demon to harm or kill the boy. An epileptic-like seizure, including falling to the ground, grinding the teeth, convulsions, and foaming at the mouth is reported. Literally, the boy is referred to as "moonstruck"; he is also described as mute.

The disciples had been unable to cast the demon from the boy. In explaining their inability, Jesus notes that their faith was inadequate. When Jesus cast out the evil spirit the boy went into convulsions. He then became so lifeless that those around him thought him dead. Here we learn that epileptic-like seizures may occur under demonic influence. We also observe again evidence of self-injury attributed to the demon. Finally, deliverance requires at least a modicum of faith.

Other New Testament Accounts

In addition to the accounts in the Gospels, there is one account of demonization in Acts, that of the fortune-telling slave girl of Philippi (Acts 16:9–21). Also, there are the accounts of Simon of Samaria (Acts 8:5–24) in which supernatural abilities are manifested, and the story of the sons of Sceva, who unsuccessfully attempted to free a person from evil spirits (Acts 19:11–17). We will examine each of these accounts.

The Slave Girl in Philippi The slave girl at Philippi possessed a spirit of divination, enabling her to make predictions about future events. She was a source of great profit to her owners because of her ability to tell fortunes. The slave girl made a habit of following Paul and his companions about the city and calling out, "'These men are bond-servants of the Most High God, who are proclaiming to you the way of salvation'" (Acts 16:17).

Her statement about Paul and his fellow-missionaries apparently reflects supernatural knowledge. Her revelation was truthful, but it is doubtful that her declarations caused many Philippians to recognize that Paul and Silas represented "the Most High God." It seems likely that her revelations, though true, nonetheless detracted from the effectiveness of Paul's and Silas's preaching. Paul ultimately commanded the spirit to come out of the girl, and an uproar ensued because the girl's masters recognized they had lost the income which they received from her fortune-telling ability.

The primary feature we discover in this account is that the demonized slave girl had supernatural knowledge that was a source of material benefit to her owners. It is noteworthy, however, that the demon did not enable her to gain her own freedom from her masters.

Simon of Samaria Philip took the gospel to Samaria, performing signs, casting unclean spirits out of many, and healing many others who were lame and paralyzed (Acts 8:5–24).

In Samaria there was a man named Simon who practiced the arts of magic; he claimed to be someone great, and the people referred to him as "the Great Power of God." Simon was among those who believed the gospel, and he apparently gave up his magic. Then, when he saw the power of the Holy Spirit manifested in Peter, he offered silver to buy this power. But Peter sternly rebuked him, and Simon apparently repented of his desire for power.

In this account we find no indication of whether Simon was influenced by a demon. It is possible that he was merely an evil person. However, the manifestation of supernatural powers at least raises the possibility that, like many of his countrymen, he, too, was demonized.

The Sons of Sceva While Paul was at Ephesus he was involved in the working of numerous signs and wonders, including healing the sick and casting out evil spirits. Even handkerchiefs and aprons brought to Paul and then taken to the afflicted resulted in such healings (Acts 19:9–17). Some itinerant Jewish exorcists who happened to be in Ephesus, hearing of Paul's miraculous doings, also sought to cast out evil spirits in the name of "Jesus whom Paul preaches." The sons of Sceva, a Jewish chief priest, sought to do this on a particular occasion, with dismaying results:

> And the evil spirit answered and said to them, "I recognize Jesus, and I know about Paul, but who are you?" And the man, in whom was the evil spirit, leaped on them and subdued both of them and overpowered them, so that they fled out of that house naked and wounded.
>
> (Acts 19:15–16)

In this episode we are reminded of the power and ferocity of persons influenced by demons. Further, invoking the name of Jesus, as such, is not adequate for exorcising all demons. One must also have a personal relationship with God through Jesus.

OTHER BIBLICAL ACCOUNTS OF DEMONIC ACTIVITIES

In addition to the above accounts of overt demonization, there are a number of additional biblical stories that shed light on Satan's nature and work. In the Old Testament, these include the story of the Fall in the Garden of Eden, the encounter between Moses and the magicians and sorcerers of Egypt, and Daniel's encounters with the astrologers and Chaldeans of Babylon.

In the New Testament, the parable of the sower is of interest (Matt. 13:3–23), the parable of the wheat and the tares (Matt. 13:24–30), and the confrontation between Jesus and the Pharisees regarding their unbelief, in John 8:31–48. Other New Testament reports of Satan include brief glimpses of his character in the New Testament Epistles, and prophetic glimpses into his activities as represented by the passages that speak of the dragon, the beast, and the false prophet in Revelation.

Old Testament Accounts

The Garden of Eden The first recorded interaction between Satan and humans is found in Genesis 3. Here Satan is referred to merely as "the serpent," but it is widely agreed that this is Satan

43

himself in disguised form.[7] The serpent first asked a seemingly innocuous question. He then flatly contradicted God's instruction, and followed with an appeal to the desire to be like God:

> And the serpent said to the woman, "You surely shall not die! For God knows that in the day you eat from it your eyes will be opened, and you will be like God, knowing good and evil."
> (Gen. 3:4–5)

Satan's guile and his lying are revealed in this encounter with Eve.

Moses and the Egyptians In Moses' encounter with Pharaoh, seeking the freedom of Israel from Egyptian slavery, Pharaoh's magicians and sorcerers were able to duplicate some of the miracles which God performed at the hands of Moses. They were able to cause their rods to turn into snakes, water to turn to blood, and frogs to spring forth on the land. However, when Moses and Aaron turned the dust to gnats, and they could not, "Then the magicians said to Pharaoh, 'This is the finger of God'" (Exod. 8:19). It appears that while the magicians had remarkable powers, they recognized that their powers were limited.

Daniel and the Chaldeans Though less is reported about them, it seems probable that the Chaldeans, magicians, sorcerers, diviners, and conjurers of Babylon used occult powers similar to those of Pharaoh's magicians and sorcerers to accomplish their work (see Daniel 2, 5). Evidently, they had considerable power to explain dreams and to interpret inscriptions.

New Testament Accounts

The Parable of the Sower In this familiar account Jesus used an analogy regarding sowing grain to teach principles regarding the kingdom of heaven. When the grain was sown, some seed fell on the path and was consumed by the birds, some fell on rocky ground that lacked the soil to support sustained growth, some fell among thorns and was choked out, and other seed dropped on good soil, yielding a crop of greater or lesser bounty.

In explaining the parable, Jesus says that seed sown by the road and eaten by birds represents those who hear the word of God without understanding it; then "the evil one comes and snatches away what has been sown." Seed sown on rocky ground represents those who hear the word and receive it with joy, but without the firm root of continuing commitment. When persecution or affliction comes these "fall away" because they lack the depth of sincere commitment necessary to endure criticism or opposition. Seed sown among thorns represents those who hear the Word of God with initial positive response. However, daily worries about food, shelter, and clothing, and the desire for riches, are more powerful, eventually choking out concern for obedience to God. Only those who receive the Word of the kingdom in such a way that it bears the "peaceable fruits of righteousness" truly benefit.

In this parable Satan is presented as the one who snatches way the truth of the kingdom so that it will not bear fruit in the hearts of the hearers. Satan is thus a deceiver not only in the sense that he presents lies, but also in actively seeking to hide, discredit, or take away memory of the truth. This seems to have been an important element in Satan's approach to Eve in the Garden of Eden. Similarly, it may be that the words of the slave girl of Philippi, though truthful, tended to discredit Paul and Silas; in this way they apparently served to disrupt the ministry of the gospel.

The power of the truth to deceive when taken out of context is nicely illustrated by a story I once heard. It is reported that the captain of a sailing vessel in the seventeenth century had a problem with excessive drinking. Eventually, the first mate decided to deal with the problem by making a record of it in the ship's log. From time to time he would note, "The captain was drunk tonight" in the log. On discovering this, the captain was furious and swore to get revenge. After considering for some time how he would get back at his first mate, the captain wrote a single entry in the log: "The first mate was sober tonight." Even the truth can mislead!

The Parable of the Tares This story tells of a man who planted good seed in his field. Later, when his slaves went out to check on the grain, they discovered the field so full of tares, which was a noxious weed, that they concluded that the tares had been deliberately sown in the field. They promptly reported to their

45

master, who confirmed that he had sown good seed not weeds, and charged that an enemy had sown the weeds. When asked if they should uproot the tares, the master told the slaves to wait until harvest so that the grain would not be destroyed in the process of removing the weeds.

When the disciples asked Jesus for an explanation of this parable, Jesus told them that he is the sower of the good seed, the field is the world, and the good grain represents the sons of God's kingdom. The tares are the sons of the evil one, and the enemy who sowed them is the devil. The harvest is the end of the age and the reapers are angels (Matt. 13:37–39).

In the harvest at the end of the age the tares, which represent those apart from God and within the kingdom of Satan, are to be gathered up and thrown into the lake of fire. The good grain, representing those who belong to the kingdom of God, is taken into the heavenly storehouse.

Christ's Confrontation One of the strongest reports about the character of Satan is in the words of Christ, in a confrontation with the Pharisees:

"You are of your father the devil, and you want to do the desires of your father. He was a murderer from the beginning, and does not stand in the truth, because there is no truth in him. Whenever he speaks a lie, he speaks from his own nature; for he is a liar, and the father of lies."

(John 8:44)

Prophetic Accounts In Revelation we find prophecy regarding the activities of the dragon, the beast, and the false prophet. The dragon, identified as Satan, is initially pictured in heaven. There he wars against Michael and his angels, is defeated, and is cast down to the earth. The dragon is pictured as seeking to destroy a woman and her child, presumably Christ. Failing this, the dragon then makes war against the rest of her offspring, those "who keep the commandments of God and hold to the testimony of Jesus" (Rev. 12:17).

The beast is given power and great authority by the dragon, but suffers a fatal injury; the dragon demonstrates miraculous

46

powers, healing the beast's incurable wound. As a result, the dragon and the beast become objects of fear and worship. They set themselves up against God and his people, making war against the saints. A second beast appears, also manifesting miraculous powers; he compels the whole earth to worship the first beast and to receive the mark of the beast on their right hands or foreheads (Rev. 12, 13).

When given permission by God, Satan is able to destroy the human body. At Corinth, the man who was involved in gross sexual immorality was turned over to Satan for the destruction of the body so that his spirit might be preserved (see 1 Corinthians 5:1–5). It appears that only God has the power to destroy the soul or spirit (Matt. 10:28–29; Heb. 10:31). This power over men's souls which God has involves his exercise of divine judgment and the ability to assign those who do not have their names recorded in the book of life to the lake of fire; this is the second (or spiritual) death (see Revelation 20:11–15).

Satan actively works in the sons of disobedience. They are characterized by a life governed by the lusts and desires of the flesh and mind, and by wrath (Eph. 2:1–3). Satan himself can appear as an angel of light, as we have noted, and Satan's evil spirits are able to masquerade as ministers of the gospel and spirits of God. Thus, we are warned to test the spirits (1 John 4:1).

One indicator of a false spirit is that it does not confess that Jesus Christ has come in the flesh; furthermore, those who are of God and those of the world (hence false spirits) do not listen to each other or understand each other (see 1 John 4:1–6).

A number of other passages of Scripture shed further light on the character of Satan. We are warned to be alert because the devil "prowls about like a roaring lion, seeking someone to devour" (1 Pet. 5:8–9), and he must be resisted by faith. He is described as the accuser of the brethren (Rev. 12:10; cf. Job 1:6–12; 2:1–6) and a deceiver (Rev. 12:9; 13:14). In the letter to those at Smyrna, reference is made to "the blasphemy by those who say they are Jews and are not, but are a synagogue of Satan" (Rev. 2:8–11).

In light of Satan's power and craftiness, it is reassuring to know that nothing is able to separate us from God, not even evil spirits (see Rom. 8:37–39). Though Satan and his demons comprise a powerful kingdom, Jesus is above all rule, authority, and kingdom, and power (see 1 Cor. 15:24; Eph. 1:21; Phil. 2:5–11; and 1 Pet. 3:22).

FORMS AND EFFECTS OF DEMONIC INFLUENCE

There is much disagreement among popular evangelical writers regarding the various forms which demonic influence may take. One finds reference to demonic influence, harassment, control, oppression, obsession, and possession.[8] Because the derivation of these terms has little direct biblical basis, there is also little agreement about how they are defined. Perhaps the most literal rendering of the biblical Greek expressions is *demonized*. The expression *demonized* allows for a range of influence from that which is minimal, such as giving suggestions or planting ideas, to the more complete influence often referred to as "demon possession." Taken as a whole, the various biblical passages seem supportive of this notion of a continuum of influence. In addition, influence seems to fall broadly into two types, involving influence over the body and influence over the mind; Thiessen terms these respectively oppression and obsession.[9]

Thiessen's distinction between oppression and obsession may have merit. It is important to distinguish between demonization (or possession) and other forms of influence. However, for now we will refer to the whole range of phenomena as demonic influence. This approach will be taken for two reasons. First, because it emphasizes the fact that regardless of the form, all of these phenomena include an element of overt demonic activity. Second, while possession of Christians is disputed, there seems little doubt that Christians can be influenced by Satan and his underlings.[10]

As has been noted, biblical accounts of demonization are largely limited to the period during the life of Christ and the early apostolic era. The one possible exception is that of King Saul of Israel.

Taking these accounts as a whole, several signs of demonic influence are presented. It is noteworthy that the specific signs vary significantly from one account to another. Signs of demonic influence include:

- demonstrations of supernatural knowledge
- performance of feats of supernatural strength
- acts of magic
- symptoms of physical illness—inability to speak or to hear, blindness, epileptic seizures
- use of altered voice(s)
- absence of normal social graces—for example, going about naked; self-mutilation
- fierce and violent behavior
- bizarre behavior
- appearance of distinct and different personalities

All of these signs are examined in greater detail later.

Other things that we learn from these accounts include the discovery that demons are apparently uncomfortable in the "natural" state and desire to inhabit bodies, especially those of humans. Also, the expulsion of demons, without something to take their place, may actually lead to more serious demonization. Finally, we can see that it is dangerous to confront demons except in the power of God; they are able to defend themselves and attack the would-be exorcist.

One problem a person immediately faces in surveying the symptoms of demonic influence is that these same symptoms may occur in persons who are not demonized. Those who doubt that King Saul was demon possessed mention Saul as an example of such difficulty. Even the practice of magic, supernatural strength, and supernatural knowledge may be simulated through illusion, unusual physical powers, and access to secret knowledge. André Kole, a Christian "illusionist" and representative of Campus Crusade for Christ, has devoted his life to demonstrating this fact. Thus the mere presence of these signs, taken alone, is inadequate to assure that the person so characterized is in fact demonized.

In reflecting on this problem it is helpful to remember that Satan is a liar and deceiver. Presumably, one of his basic strategies is to confuse people regarding his presence, manifestation, and activities. Given the nature and work of Satan, this should come as no great surprise.[11]

SUMMARY

As we have seen, Satan is a living, active, and powerful adversary. One of his activities is overt demonization. However, it is quite clear from the biblical record that Satan is not limited to this mode of operation. Satan is a wily adversary who suits his tactics to the situation so that he can most effectively accomplish his purposes. There is much in Scripture that suggests that, even in the time of Christ, Satan manifested himself in many other ways as well as through overt influence or possession. The next chapter discusses this issue in greater detail.

CHAPTER FOUR

FAULTY THINKING: SEPARATING THE SPIRITUAL AND THE PHYSICAL

Satan is a wily adversary who approaches us where we are most vulnerable. If we are to be effective in combating him, we must avoid two common contemporary errors. The first is to spiritualize such issues as mental disorders, ignoring the physical aspects. The second is to materialize the problem, thus ignoring its spiritual dimensions. Each of these approaches is fundamentally reductionistic. Each contains an element of truth, yet both deny a significant aspect of reality as well. To adequately deal with the problem of the demonic we must recognize and steer clear of both of these errors.[1]

In the material which follows we will consider dualism, the concept of causality and its relationship to divine action, materialism as a worldview—and Satan's tactics, and the influence of adaptation on our awareness of satanic influence. We will also discuss the existence of two spiritual kingdoms, the role of sin in the world and the Fall, personal sinfulness, and Satan's involvement in this process. And we will briefly address the nature of persons.

DUALISM

A basic philosophical perspective within our culture is dualism, the view that reality is divided into two entities, the material and the spiritual. This view has been strongly influenced by Plato, the early Greek philosopher.

Briefly, Plato's view was that there are two worlds, the material world in which we live, and the rational world of ideas. For Plato, the material world was but a shadow of the rational world; to him the world of ideas was far more real than the material realm.[2]

In contemporary American thought, we see at least two viewpoints that are outgrowths of Platonic idealism. In one, matter is believed to be the only form of existence; reason is viewed as an epiphenomenon, something that occurs only as an extension of the material essence and that cannot exist without the material. This view, common among atheists and agnostics, involves materialistic reductionism, and often is referred to simply as materialism.

The second version is more common among Christians, in part as a reaction to materialism. It is the view that the immaterial is primary and the material is illusory. Many of us are influenced to some degree by this view, largely at an unconscious level.

Integral to this perspective, in the form held by some Christians, is belief in a temporal body that is inhabited by an immortal soul. This notion of an immortal soul is very close to that of Plato. It suggests that the human soul possesses the inherent capacity for eternal existence rather than depending upon God's action to grant eternal life. It also fails to recognize that in heaven believers will have physical bodies. No common terminology has developed to refer to the view underlying the notion of the immortality of the soul in Christian circles; we will call it spiritual reductionism since the simpler expression, spiritualism, has a common usage that is quite distinct. Ironically, spiritual reductionism also has strong parallels in the Eastern mystical traditions. The biblical view of man, as we shall see, involves both spiritual and material elements.[3]

Both materialism and spiritual reductionism are attempts to resolve the dilemma posed by Platonic mind-body dualism. Different forms of dualism, and especially the tendencies toward materialism and spiritualistic reductionism as a reaction to it, lie at the root of many of the thorny theological issues separating Christians. The tendency to adopt material or spiritual reductionism as a reaction to dualism is also central to the problems which we must address in order to understand clearly the relationship between mental disorders and demonic influence. Thus, an understanding of the ways in which we are affected, often unconsciously, by these forms of thought is vital to resolving the question of how to counsel those who are influenced by Satan and his demonic agents.[4]

CAUSALITY: GOD AND CREATION

Many of us have heard the arguments. They focus on whether a particular event was the result of natural processes or divine intervention. Aunt Jane was involved in a serious car accident in which she sustained severe head injuries, leaving her in a deep coma. The doctor proposed brain surgery, but the prognosis was guarded; the operation was extremely risky. Further, the doctor predicted that even if Aunt Jane survived she would be unable to function normally. With the family's consent the doctor operated. Her family, friends, and church congregation prayed fervently.

A few days later Jane showed dramatic improvement. She regained consciousness and the ability to communicate, and was able to respond to peripheral stimulation. Gradually she regained the use of her limbs.

Perhaps you can imagine the debate; you may have participated in it. The family insisted that God had miraculously healed Jane. Skeptics argued that it was the surgeon's delicate, highly developed skills which accounted for her healing. How would you answer?

R. J. Ritzema, in a study of causal attribution, presents some intriguing data which highlights this question. Ritzema asked people to account for unpleasant events; they were to choose from explanations in terms of naturalistic factors or explanations in terms of God's intervention. He found that where naturalistic reasons could be found, people tended to use those reasons to account for events. When no natural reasons were available, supernatural ones were suggested. His findings suggest that naturalistic and supernaturalistic accounts are viewed as competing alternatives.[5]

It is noteworthy that Ritzema apparently did not provide the opportunity to respond with an explanation that included *both* God's action and natural processes. Yet it is precisely such a response that appears to be most consistent with Scripture.

We must begin with the recognition that God created our world, including all of its laws and processes (Gen. 1, 2; John 1:3; Col. 1:16). Moreover, God sustains the world in existence continuously by his mighty power (see Hebrews 1:2–4 and Colossians 1:15–19; God not only created all things, but all things depend moment by moment on his sustaining power). Thus, we must recognize that no event, even a "natural one," can occur without God's personal involvement.

God's involvement may be direct and personal, as in creating the heavens and the earth, or in speaking to Moses out of the burning bush. It may also be indirect, as in sending the rain and snow from heaven to water the earth, with the result of providing seed to the sower and bread to the eater (see Isa. 55:10; Matt. 5:45). We must recognize that God is involved regardless of the specific method he employs. God's sovereignty over the earth is so complete that not a sparrow falls to the ground without his knowledge and involvement (Matt. 10:29–31; Luke 12:6–7). Even the hairs of our heads do not escape his notice. Everything that lives, breathes, moves, and exists in all of creation does so only because God wills and enables it to do so. God is involved in every event in creation!

To return to Aunt Jane, it poses a false dichotomy, then, to ask whether God healed her or she recovered because of the surgery. God healed her. This is equally true whether God used the skill of the surgeon, the "miracles" of anesthesia and pain medication, and the remarkable recuperative powers of the human body—which God made to accomplish this end—or whether he used an extraordinary and miraculous process. The appropriate question is not whether God healed Jane, but how he did it.

This tendency to view God and natural causes as competing explanations for events in our world is an outgrowth of dualistic thinking. A related outgrowth of dualism is the custom of referring to our world as "nature." While often not a conscious process, referring to our universe as nature subtly suggests that it just "naturally" occurred rather than coming from divine origins. James Houston has suggested that the word *nature* is alien to a biblical worldview.[6] The Bible refers to our world as "creation."[7]

Distinguishing between creation and nature may seem like hair-splitting. However, it becomes clear on closer reflection that this seemingly superficial distinction has profound and far-reaching implications for us.

Use of the term *nature* suggests that the world came into being through an impersonal process. Thus, the tendency to think and talk of nature subtly biases our thinking toward the dualistic view of events which we have just discussed. By contrast, the word *creation* suggests that God is at work even in everyday events. Thinking of our world as creation calls to mind the existence of a Creator and the act of creation. This is consistent with the teaching of Scripture that God created our world and that he sustains it in its operation moment to moment.

MATERIALISM AND SATAN'S TACTICS

We have already noted that one of the problems we must face in understanding the role of the demonic in mental illness is our tendency to view the world in a dualistic way, and the accompanying tendency to simplify this duality by adopting either materialism or spiritualistic reductionism. Both of these approaches are reductionistic, and, to the degree that they are adopted, reflect a distortion of reality.

Perhaps partly in response to the rampant materialism in our contemporary Western culture, Christians have commonly chosen to emphasize the spiritual dimension. In some respects this view is reactionary. Unfortunately, there are many negative ramifications to this almost exclusively spiritualistic focus. One is the tendency to regard all that is spiritual as God's responsibility. This results in looking to God to make us holy apart from our action rather than recognizing that as co-laborers we are to work out our own salvation (sanctification) even as God works in us toward that end.

A second negative ramification of spiritualistic reductionism is the contemporary tendency to find demons in every form of human evil from anger to zoophilia. The key problem with this view is that it implicitly denies that the material order has any significance. Thus mental disorders tend to be viewed exclusively in spiritual terms. It also minimizes or denies that humans bear the marks of the Fall, and consequently have an inherent propensity toward sin. This approach subtly undermines any personal responsibility for the individual's present condition, and implies that there is little the person can do to change his or her condition except petition God to act miraculously, outside the ongoing processes which sustain this world.

In the interest of maintaining a balanced perspective, it is important to remember that those who doubt the existence of demons, or perhaps believe that they are simply irrelevant, commit the opposite error of materialistic reductionism. This view denies the reality that we are engaged in a war involving the spiritual forces of darkness and light.[8]

ADAPTATION AND AWARENESS OF SATANIC INFLUENCE

Another problem is the fact that we tend to become insensitive to Satan's most prevalent forms of activity within our culture. It is much easier to recognize satanic activity in cultures which are radically different from ours because we have not become adapted to the point that we are unable to detect them. We are easily lulled into complacency by the familiar. Satan is able to act more freely, without as much fear of detection, when his activities are consistent with our worldviews.

Modern information-processing theorists consider adaptation a basic function of cognitive processing. According to this view, our nervous system is designed in such a way that it responds to changes in stimulus events. When a new stimulus event occurs we respond to it. Similarly, if a stimulus event terminates, we respond to this change as well. However, in the presence of a constant stimulus we soon cease to respond; it's almost as if the stimulus weren't there. Put differently, if a stimulus continues long enough we come to ignore it. Even a fire alarm, if it sounds continuously, soon ceases to produce a response.

The tendency to respond to changes in stimulus events is illustrated by the reaction of persons who have grown accustomed to the 2:15 A.M. train passing nightly on the tracks 150 yards from their home. Over time they learn to sleep through this nightly occurrence, never even knowing that it happens. Then, when the schedule changes, they awaken with a start at 2:15 A.M., certain that something is wrong.

Satan's familiar tactics are rather like the passage of that train. We become so accustomed to them we do not even notice. But when we observe an unfamiliar pattern, perhaps from a different culture, it prompts our notice. Going to another country where occult practices are common, we are confronted with a pattern which is unfamiliar and immediately smacks of evil. I'm told by people who come from other cultures that they likewise find some aspects of evil in our society quite blatant, though they have typically become unaware of the patterns of evil in their own cultures.

I believe that overt demonic influence is an exception, not a customary mode of Satan's activity in our contemporary society. Satan's normal approach is much more subtle. He most often acts in ways that are consistent with the widespread naturalism and materialistic reductionism of contemporary Western thinking. By approaching those who hold materialistic worldviews in ways consistent with those views, Satan avoids drawing attention toward his activities and involvement. In a culture such as ours which views everything in naturalistic terms and denies the reality of the spiritual, this approach is apparently much more effective for accomplishing his ungodly objectives than the more open and direct approach of overt demonic influence.

Two Kingdoms

From a spiritual perspective we may think of each person as belonging to one of two kingdoms, the kingdom of God, or the kingdom of "the god of this world," Satan (2 Cor. 4:4).

In his discussion with Nicodemus, Jesus suggested the need to be born again. Nicodemus was perplexed. Jesus explained that as a natural man, Nicodemus was born into sin. As a direct consequence, Jesus went on, Nicodemus was "condemned already" because he was not involved in a believing, saving relationship with God through Jesus Christ. Jesus' comments make it clear that there are only two possibilities: either we have been condemned already or we have entered into a saving relationship with God (John 3:1–18). In this and other contexts Jesus declares that anyone who is not with him is against him (see Matt. 12:30; Mark 9:39–40; Luke 9:49–50; 11:14–23).

The thesis of two kingdoms is developed further in Paul's discussion of attitudes regarding meat sacrificed to idols (1 Cor. 8:1–13). Paul suggests that idols themselves are of no account; thus eating meat sacrificed to idols is, of itself, not a problem. However, some believers, those referred to as "weaker brethren," because of their past experience with the worship of idols, do not know this fully; Paul describes this condition by noting that their conscience is weak. When Paul returns to this discussion, however, he takes it one step further. He notes that "the things which the Gentiles sacrifice, they sacrifice to demons . . ." (1 Cor. 10:20). This further underscores the truth that there are only two spiritual kingdoms in this world, the kingdom of God and the kingdom of Satan.

It is no accident that Satan is referred to as the god of this age. It is suggested here that all false worship is ultimately worship of Satan, though often this is unwittingly so on the part of the worshiper.

In chapter 6 of Romans Paul addresses this issue somewhat differently. He describes the person in a fallen condition as a slave to sin. Through identification with Christ in the process of salvation and union with him we become dead to sin and free from this slavery. What is striking is that Paul then exhorts us to reckon (or consider) ourselves as dead to sin and alive to righteousness. Then we are to present ourselves to God as "weapons" of righteousness. Paul sums up this argument with the stark contrast:

> Do you not know that when you present yourselves to someone as slaves for obedience, you are slaves of the one whom you obey, either of sin resulting in death, or of obedience resulting in righteousness? But thanks be to God that though you were slaves of sin, you became obedient from the heart to that form of teaching to which you were committed, and having been freed from sin, you became slaves of righteousness. (Rom. 6:16–18)

As Paul puts it, the choice is not slavery or freedom. Rather, we must choose to whom we will become enslaved: God or Satan. Moreover, we begin life enslaved to Satan. In confronting the Pharisees, Jesus approached the question of two kingdoms in a slightly different way; he said of them: "You are of your father the devil, and you want to do the desires of your father." The text makes it clear that Jesus was saying that the Pharisees had the same nature or essential character as Satan. By contrast, when one receives Christ he or she becomes a new creature because God's seed is in him or her (see 2 Cor. 5:17; 1 John 3:1–2, 9).

According to these passages, all who are outside of the household of faith are by their very nature oriented to doing Satan's will. Furthermore, they are unable to do God's will (Heb. 11:6). Such individuals are influenced by Satan at their very core. In most instances no overt demonic influence is manifested in their lives. Yet Satan's influence flows from their innermost being, from their very hearts.

The notion of two kingdoms suggests that all unbelievers are members of Satan's kingdom. As members of his kingdom, they also are under his influence whether or not they recognize it. Thus we must conclude that all unbelievers are under satanic influence.

The notion of two kingdoms gains further support in Colossians when Paul describes the process of salvation in terms of a change of kingdoms:

> For He delivered us from the domain of darkness, and transferred us to the kingdom of His beloved Son, in whom we have redemption, the forgiveness of sin.
>
> (Col. 1:13–14)

It is important to recognize, however, that the Christian is not removed from the exposure to satanic influence. The struggle with sin and Satan continues throughout this earthly life.

Numerous biblical passages, such as those telling of Eve, Judas, Jesus himself, Peter, and others further underscore the fact that Satan's kingdom is powerful and pervasive, affecting even the believer.

Eve and Satan   When Satan approached Eve in the Garden of Eden, he clearly influenced her decision to disobey God by eating of the fruit of the tree of the knowledge of good and evil. This was accomplished through dialogue, rather than through physical control such as we customarily associate with demonic influence. Nonetheless, the evidence that Eve was influenced by Satan is compelling (see Gen. 3).

Judas   Judas was the "treasurer" for the disciples and Jesus; he kept the moneybag. In this office he was apparently less than scrupulously honest (see John 12:3–6). Doubtless, in this transgression Judas was influenced by Satan to some degree.

At the time of the Last Supper we are told that the devil had put it into Judas' heart to betray Jesus (John 13:2). Just prior to the betrayal "Satan entered into Judas" (Luke 22:1–3ff.; John 13:27). "Entered" means, literally or figuratively, to enter, or to come in. Regardless of how one interprets the expression "entered into," it is clear that Judas was under the influence of Satan at the time of the betrayal.

Jesus   Even Jesus was not exempt from the advances of Satan. At the beginning of his preparation for earthly ministry, Jesus went away into the desert and fasted for forty days and nights. At the end of this period Satan came to him, apparently in a physical presence, and tempted him to sin in three distinct ways. He challenged Jesus to change stones into bread, to jump off the temple roof and demand that God protect him, and to attempt to gain access to all the kingdoms of the world and their attendant glory prematurely.

These temptations appear to address the three major areas of potential for human sin, named in 1 John 2:16–18: the lust of the flesh (food needed for bodily sustenance after prolonged fasting), the lust of the eyes (earthly kingdoms), and the pride of life (an egotistical attempt to compel God's protection). No one would describe this experience as one of demon possession. Jesus did not succumb, but it is clear that Satan was active in seeking to influence him.

Peter In the life of Peter two episodes are recorded in which he was influenced by Satan. When Jesus first began to teach his disciples about the fact that he must suffer and die, Peter took Jesus aside and rebuked him, saying this should never happen to him. At that time Jesus said to Peter, "'Get behind me, Satan! You are a stumbling block to Me; for you are not setting your mind on God's interests, but man's'" (Matt. 16:23; cp. Mark 8:30–33). Ryrie notes, "Peter was used by Satan to try to dissuade Jesus from going to the cross."[9] It seems that Satan's goal on these occasions was to influence Christ through Peter.

On the evening of the crucifixion, after dinner and just before going out to the Mount of Olives, the disciples fell into a discussion of who among them was the greatest (see Luke 22:24ff.). Jesus responded to this discussion, turning to Peter and telling him: "Simon, Simon, behold, Satan has demanded permission to sift you like wheat; but I have prayed for you that your faith may not fail; and you, when once you have turned again, strengthen your brothers" (Luke 22:31–32). Jesus then went on to warn Peter that he would deny Jesus three times before the cock crowed. In this interaction it appears that Jesus gave permission to Satan to have extensive influence over Peter, limited by Jesus' prayer that God would protect Peter's faith.

Two other events in Peter's life may evidence the activity of Satan or demons in influencing his conduct. First, when Jesus was transfigured in his presence, Peter proposed that they build tabernacles for Jesus, Moses, and Elijah. Had this been done, it could have distracted Jesus from his earthly mission. Second, in the Garden of Gethsemane, when the soldiers came to arrest Jesus, Peter began to fight against them with a sword. Again, Peter's action was inconsistent with God's plan, and may have been the result of evil influence.

Although we do not have adequate space to develop the accounts (in some instances less detail is provided), many other persons in Scripture clearly were under satanic influence. Among these were Ahab and Jezebel, Pharoah and his magicians, Cain, the astrologers and Chaldeans of Babylon, and King Darius.

THE FALL, AND SIN IN THE WORLD

We have examined the role of Satan at some length. While it is not the purpose of our discussion to dwell here on the Fall and consequent entrance of sin into our world, it is nonetheless important to acknowledge that Adam and Eve set in motion a sequence of events with far-reaching implications. For our purposes, two of these need to be emphasized: first, the fact that spiritual death or separation from God, together with the predisposition to personal sin, became the lot of all mankind; second, all of creation was dramatically altered.

Personal Sinfulness

Because of the Fall, sin and death became the lot of all mankind. It is hard to comprehend all of the implications of this simple fact. As Jay Adams notes, in the Genesis 3 account we immediately discover fear, shame, deception, and blame-shifting.[10]

The wages of sin is death, we are told (Rom. 3:23). Death is multifaceted: immediate separation from God, eventual physical death, and potentially the "second death," or eternal separation from God.[11]

Because of the transgression of Adam and Eve, the predisposition to personal sinfulness is built into each of us. As we shall see later, this fact contributes to the tendency to experience mental disorders and demonic influence.

The Sin of Others

The Fall also resulted in the sinfulness of others; each person experiences the unpleasantness of being sinned against. Our parents are imperfect, as are our brothers and sisters, friends, spouses, and children. The fact that we are the victims of sin further contributes to the problems of mental disorders and demonic influence.

Sin in the World

Beyond the effects of personal sin and the sins of others, the entrance of sin into our world had profound effects on all of Creation. We are told that "the whole creation groans and suffers" waiting to be set free with the children of God (Rom. 8:18–23). It is hard to grasp all of the implications of this cataclysmic change. It appears that predation, one animal killing another for food, is a result of the Fall. Also, disease, natural disaster, and similar things are all effects of the Fall; mental disorders are another of the many facets of this groaning and suffering. Although it is appealing to attribute all mental disorders to personal sin, we must recognize that the profound disturbance of the Fall makes matters far more complicated. Chapters 5 and 6 further develop this thinking.

SATAN'S ROLE IN THE SEPARATION OF THE SPIRITUAL AND PHYSICAL

The tendency toward dualistic thinking, and the accompanying tendencies toward materialism and spiritual reductionism are not merely human misconceptions. We must also understand that they are among the many consequences of spiritual warfare. Though not really quite so simple, in one sense all such misconceptions are the result of a *diabolical* plot. Full, true worship of God is precluded by either form of reductionism.

Carried to its logical conclusion, materialism denies the very existence of God. It may seem less readily apparent, but spiritual reductionism is no less atheistic; while acknowledging God in a mystical, spiritualistic way, it denies the full physical, daily reality of his majestic, creative, and redemptive acts. It denies that God became flesh and dwelt among us (John 1:14), and that God's plan includes the redemption and transformation of our physical bodies.

Because naturalistic materialism is so widespread in our culture, it seems not at all surprising that Satan tends to present himself in ways consistent with this worldview so as not to draw attention to himself. To put himself in the spotlight would draw attention to the spiritual realm, thus inevitably also drawing attention to the reality of God. For those who discount God, this might direct their attention toward him. For those who already believe in God, such overt manifestation would alert them to seek God's resources for defense against spiritual attack.

Does it not make sense that Satan's preferred mode of action is to use more natural means, perhaps such activities as alcohol and drug abuse, sexual obsessions, gambling, preoccupation with wealth, "things," or status, rather than overt demonization? These are no less enslaving, no less damaging, and no less forms of satanic influence because they are not openly "spiritual."

THE NATURE OF PERSONS

Although space cannot be devoted to developing the subject in detail, a few comments about the nature of persons are essential at this point.

Humans are created beings, made in the image of God, and fallen. We are told that God created Adam out of the dust of the ground, and breathed into him the breath of life. Persons were created both male and female. Though it is subject to some disagreement among scholars, the image of God suggests that persons are unique in creation as spiritual, mental, moral and social beings. After his creation, God gave humans dominion over the earth. Taken together, the facts of (1) the image of God and (2) dominion give humans a dignity of being and breadth of responsibility accorded to no other creature.

Initially, Adam and Eve existed in untested holiness. However, they transgressed God's command. As a result, sin and death passed on all mankind. This death has three aspects: spiritual, physical, and eternal. The salvation provided in Jesus Christ involves restoration of spiritual life and escape from eternal death into eternal life. However, the judgment of physical death continues to be carried out on all persons. This process, too, is reversed in the re-creation of individuals at the resurrection.[12]

The existence of mental disorders, indeed of all natural evil, can be traced to the fact of sin. As we shall see, mental disorders involve elements of sin in the world, the sin of others, and personal sin.

Persons are units or wholes. For analytic purposes it is helpful to view persons as composed of parts: material and spiritual, or body and soul, in the common dichotomous view; body, mind, and soul in the trichotomous view. One of the effects of dualistic thinking is the tendency to view the eternal state as one of eternal spiritual existence, in the absence of the material aspects of our beings.[13] However, it is clear in Scripture that we will be whole beings, comprised of spiritual and physical dimensions in heaven (see 1 Corinthians 15:12–21, 39–58; 2 Cor. 5:1–5; cp. John 14:1–3). Thus, we must affirm again that humans are whole beings comprised of material and spiritual; we are psychospiritual and material unities.

SUMMARY

To fully grasp the issues involved in satanic and demonic influence it is important to understand the subtle and pervasive effects of dualism on contemporary thought. Dualism is the tendency to view reality as composed of two parts, material and spiritual, rather than as a unified whole with two inseparable aspects.

Because of dualistic thinking we tend to view spiritual and natural explanations of events such as healings as competing explanations rather than as compatible explanations at different levels of analysis. Similarly, we tend to see Satan and demons as active only in overt "spiritualistic" phenomena which take the form of influence and "possession," discounting satanic involvement in "natural" events such as a traffic accident.

Spiritually, there are only two kingdoms, the kingdom of God and Satan's kingdom. Each person belongs to one of these, as is illustrated by several biblical accounts. Satan constantly wars against God and those who choose to enter into his kingdom.

Satan is a wily warrior who uses those stratagems that most effectively accomplish his ends. Thus he adapts his approaches to fit within a given culture's prevailing worldview; in this way we become adapted to his approaches and they escape detection—and thus his designs are more effective. Toward this end, Satan fosters and encourages dualistic thinking. Accordingly, in contemporary Western culture Satan's approaches fit within a naturalistic, materialistic framework to escape our notice.

CHAPTER FIVE

MENTAL ILLNESS

Defining mental illness is not an easy task. Much controversy swirls around the definition, and even around whether "mental illness" is a helpful concept. The use of the word *illness* implies that some form of disease is the root of the problem. This issue lies at the heart of a major conceptual controversy in the mental health field.

Szasz called mental illness a myth.[1] Others describe mental illness in terms of several "models."[2] These include the spiritual model, the moral model, the medical model, the sociopsychological model, and the systems model.

This chapter will begin with a case example. Then we will briefly examine each of these models, as well as the possibility of a Christian model. We will conclude with a discussion of some issues that are raised from a Christian perspective. In chapter 6 we will turn to an overview of the *Diagnostic and Statistical Manual of Mental Disorders,* Third Edition, Revised (DSM-III-R), the most widely accepted manual for cataloguing the nature and types of mental disorders.[3]

JENNIFER

"My name's not Jennifer; she left. I'm Gina. That dumb slob Jennifer is gone. Good riddance. I can't have any fun when she's around." As I looked at the woman my confusion must have been apparent. I was sure it was Jennifer. Yet her clothes, her expression, her voice, her posture—almost everything about her—seemed different. I almost believed that I was speaking with the wrong woman.

When I'd seen her the day before, Jennifer was severely depressed, suicidal. She had been hospitalized for fear that she would kill herself. Before admission, she had been systematically slashing her arm with a razor; the mutilated skin on her left arm hung in ribbons. Now it was all bandaged, and hidden under the sleeves of her low-cut, seductive blouse. She wanted a pass so that she could "go out and have some fun."

As I came to know Jennifer/Gina better, I discovered that there were other "personalities" as well. They came and went unpredictably. Each had a characteristic pattern of mood and behavior. Yet all shared the same body. Jennifer was prim and proper, always doing the correct thing. Gina was fun-loving and outgoing, but irresponsible. Mae was a clever thief who managed to steal things Gina enjoyed, but which were an embarrassment to Jennifer, who could not understand how the items came into her possession. Polly was a boozing babe who would tumble into any man's bed "just for a lark."

As I pondered my experience with Jennifer, I reflected on the various ways to view her "personalities." Surely she had a mental illness, a multiple-personality disorder, together with depression, I thought. Or could she be acting? In some of her personalities she clearly engaged in various forms of sinful conduct; could it be that she was just a clever but sinful woman who had found out how to get away with doing as she pleased?

Or was she demon possessed? As we work through this and following chapters our goal is to better understand how to resolve such questions.

MODELS OF MENTAL DISORDERS

The Spiritual Model

From antiquity until the nineteenth century, mental disorders were viewed largely as a religious and moral issue. Persons with unusual behavior were considered malingerers or possessed by spirits. If the spirits were viewed as good, the person was accorded status and favor, and no efforts were made to remove their influence. By contrast, if the spirits were considered bad, exorcism and torture were used as ways to free the person from their influence. Jennifer probably would have undergone exorcism or torture.

The Moral Model

In the late eighteenth and nineteenth centuries a number of changes took place in the treatment of the mentally ill. At the beginning of this era the mentally ill were housed in large asylums. One such asylum was Bethlehem Hospital of London, from which we get the corruption "bedlam." Late in the eighteenth century, reformers such as Philippe Pinel, William Tuke, and Dorothea Dix led efforts for reform and the provision of more humanitarian care in these asylums.

In the United States this reform movement was most fully developed in the "moral treatment" approach which was most prominent at the beginning of the nineteenth century. This approach included an emphasis on small institutions of less than 250 patients. The superintendent was a father figure to the patients. Curability of mental illness was stressed, and treatment emphasized training in appropriate moral conduct. At the time, this approach was believed by some to be curative, though others disputed this claim.[4] Under the moral model, Jennifer would have received training in moral conduct in a small institution.

The Medical Model

About the same time as the humanitarian reforms and moral treatment were being practiced, Wilhelm Greisinger and Benedict Morel, among others, were involved in an effort to advance the disease notion of mental disorders. John Gray, editor of the *American Journal of Insanity* from 1855 to 1885, was a strong crusader in support of the disease view. He used his prominent role to advance the notion that physical lesions were responsible for mental illness, and he led in the movement to transform mental asylums into treatment facilities.

The theoretical work of Jean Charcot, Pierre Janet, Hippolyte Marie Bernheim, and Sigmund Freud gave further impetus to the development of the medical model. According to the moral model, persons whose symptoms did not make anatomical sense were thought to be unwilling to face the difficulties of life, and hence morally defective. Because of the work of the medical pioneers, they came to be seen as hysterics who were presumed to have medical rather than moral problems. In this way the medical model was extended to persons outside institutional settings.

A major factor giving further credence to the medical model was the discovery that general paresis, a psychotic disorder, was the result of advanced syphilitic infection. The initial suggestion was made in 1857; positive identification of syphilitic infection as the causative agent was provided in 1913. This significant discovery, together with the growing inclination to view other problems as medical, culminated in a major shift in viewpoints: The disease model replaced the moral-religious explanation of mental disorders.

The medical model, in its various forms, has been the dominant conceptual model from 1915 to the present. Although several alternative models have been proposed, none has received the widespread acceptance which the moral-religious model enjoyed before the nineteenth century, or which the medical model has been given in the twentieth century.

Blaney[5] has suggested four variations of the medical model:

1) mental disorders are in fact diseases which are physiologically based;

2) symptoms of mental disorder are reflections of an underlying condition which may be organic, but need not be so;

69

3) mental disorders are not under personal control, and the individual has no responsibility for his or her behavior;

4) psychiatric symptoms can be best understood by ordering them into syndromes, or groups of symptoms which normally occur together so that each syndrome or group of symptoms can be viewed as a single disorder.

As we shall see later, none of these definitions seems adequate to encompass all of the disorders listed in the *Diagnostic and Statistical Manual of Mental Diseases.*

The medical model assumes the person with the disorder is a patient who is sick. The sickness is characterized by a number of symptoms which are presumed to be the result of an underlying disease having a specific cause or etiology. Because the underlying problem is often not apparent, diagnosis is important prior to treatment. The illness is presumed to have a predictable developmental history or course, and prognosis or outcome.

Symptoms are presumed to be indicators of the underlying illness. They may change or even disappear without the illness being cured. Thus, identifying the disease and evaluating the effect of treatment requires special training, and becomes a medical specialty. Other concerns include the possibility of relapse or of symptom substitution, which is the development of new symptoms stemming from the same underlying ailment. Since the individual is often unable to provide basic self-care, society provides care for him or her.

The illness model takes away personal responsibility; since the patient cannot do much about the condition, the patient becomes a passive recipient of treatment.

The patient may receive special considerations such as financial support or care provided by the state. Legal rights may be lost since the person is presumed to be unable to make responsible choices. Sometimes the person is not held responsible for legal infractions. These are thought to be the result of the disease process; it is assumed that the patient did not know what he or she was doing, or did not recognize that the actions were wrong. In some respects the problem may be even more complicated; patients are believed to be incapable of evaluating their own conditions, and may not even recognize that they have problems. Alternatively, the patient may recognize the presence of a problem, but may misidentify it. In some instances, the denial of a problem is taken as evidence that the problem is more severe than if it were recognized. People like Jennifer would likely be committed to large mental hospitals under the medical model, often for extended periods of time.

Under the medical model, research and treatment are medical specialties. A concept of health must be developed against which illness is measured. Research focuses on a search for physical causes such as infections, genetic anomalies, or endocrinological abnormalities. A radical discontinuity is presumed to exist between health and disease, thus research focuses on patients; study of normal individuals is presumed to be irrelevant.

In evaluating the medical model we should recognize that it is the most widely accepted formulation at the present time. The medical model clearly underlies the early versions of the American Psychiatric Association's *Diagnostic and Statistical Manual*,[6] although later editions include some recognition of alternative models.[7]

Many mental disorders clearly fit the medical model. Among these are general paresis, the organic brain syndromes, and some cases of retardation. Clearly disease, trauma, genetic anomaly, and exposure to toxic substances can result in mental disorder. Traditionally, physical disorders such as irritable bowel syndrome, spastic colitis, ulcerative colitis and a variety of related gastrointestinal disorders were listed among the mental disorders because they were thought to be caused by psychological rather than biological factors. However, with the development of new diagnostic techniques, a number of specific biological factors have been found which account for a significant percentage of these disorders.[8] Recent evidence suggests that other mental disorders such as Alzheimer's disease and manic depressive disorders have at least a biological predisposing factor if not an outright biological cause.[9]

Despite recent findings, many mental disorders still have no known underlying disease process; Jennifer's suffering is such a disorder. It remains unclear whether further research will discover biological causes of these disorders.

Considerable difference of opinion exists regarding the contribution of the medical model. Some contend that the medical model led to the elimination of earlier abusive and inhumane methods of dealing with the mentally ill. But this view has been challenged by those who believe that the moral-treatment approach, which was replaced by the medical model, was actually responsible for more humane treatment of the mentally ill.[10]

Another criticism of the medical model is the role which it has played in the development of the legal principle of finding persons not guilty for criminal behavior because of insanity. Szasz has been a particularly outspoken critic of the model because of this effect. Thus, in some quarters the medical model is viewed as a backward step.

The Sociopsychological Model

The sociopsychological model, closely related to earlier behavioral models, is probably the most widely accepted alternative to the medical view. Where the medical model suggests qualitative distinctions between normal and disturbed functioning, the sociopsychological model contends that disordered behavior follows the same principles as normal behavior. Disordered behavior results from unusual learning experiences rather than from a disease process. Problem behavior develops by the same principles as normal behavior, and thus may be changed through application of the principles of normal learning and behavior control.

The sociopsychological model suggests that diagnosis should focus on identification of the frequencies, topographies (or forms), and social or environmental controlling conditions of problem behaviors. It assumes that the average individual is sufficiently aware of the problem to be motivated to seek change and to become an active participant in the change process. Since the person's behavior is believed to follow the normal laws of behavior, the individual is neither exculpated from social consequences nor given special privileges. Under this model the counselor would seek to discover the patterns of behavior associated with Jennifer's different "personalities" and the circumstances in which they occurred. The counselor would then seek to develop more constructive ways for Jennifer to deal with the events of her life, and to weaken or eliminate all the "personalities" except "Jennifer."

Research under the sociopsychological model focuses on discovering the principles of behavior acquisition, control, and elimination, rather than on identifying disease processes.

The sociopsychological model is based on the accumulated results of over seventy-five years of laboratory research on learning, motivation, perception, social relations, growth, and development. The basic principles of behavior are well established, and there is much evidence that therapy approaches based on this model can be very effective.[11]

Systems Model

Another model that has gained considerable support in the past few years is the systems model. This view holds that mental disorders arise out of disturbances in the family system or social system rather than from a disease or disturbed learning pattern. In this model the focus is on the interactions among members in a social system rather than on an "identified patient." Although the parents may come seeking help for a disturbed child, it is believed that the problem does not lie solely within the child; rather, the problem arises out of the interaction between the parents and the child. The problem may be affected by other individuals as well, such as siblings, extended family, and peers.

Intervention with this model is focused on changing the properties of the system rather than on changing the individual. For example, instead of directing efforts toward eliminating stealing by the second child, treatment might seek to resolve chronic conflict between the parents. According to the family-systems view, the child steals in order to keep the family together; while involved in dealing with him, Mom and Dad do not fight with each other. Thus if Mom and Dad ceased fighting, stealing would no longer be necessary.[12]

For Jennifer, this model suggests examination of her family or living situation, then seeking to alter operation of the overall system, thus changing Jennifer.

The Christian Model

Dissatisfied with the medical model, and concerned with many anti-Christian implications in the other models, some have proposed development of Christian models. During the 1970s, for example, there were a number of efforts to develop a Christian approach to counseling. Implicit in each of these is a view of mental illness or psychopathology.

Despite these efforts, it seems unlikely that there will be a single Christian approach to counseling, or a universally accepted Christian view of mental illness.[13] This is not too surprising. Just as there are many different Christian theologies and approaches to the understanding of Scripture, it seems likely that there will continue to be many Christian approaches to counseling and mental illness.[14]

Although differences seem inevitable, there are some distinctive emphases which characterize the various efforts to develop a Christian model. Almost all believers share these convictions: first, that persons have a spiritual dimension because we are all made in the image of God, and second, that mankind is fallen as a result of sin. These two factors have profound implications for a Christian approach to mental illness.

The spiritual dimension is believed to provide a resource which can prevent or ameliorate mental disorders. Also, many Christian authors believe that at least some mental disorders come about because the spiritual dimension is neglected, or is distorted through sin.[15] If this view is correct, then a complete and fully effective approach to treating mental disorders must include the use of spiritual resources such as forgiveness, repentance, prayer, and Scripture.

Despite general agreement in some areas, there are other areas of disagreement among Christian authors. For example, consider the different views about the relationship between theological and psychological approaches to knowledge.

At one extreme on this issue are those who agree with Ellens:

> Since Christians acknowledge that all truth is God's truth, no matter who finds it or where it is found, the information derived from both psychology and theology is taken with equal seriousness. God's message in the special revelation of Scripture and God's general revelation in the created world are both sought diligently to ensure the maximum constructive interaction between theology and psychology.[16]

Carter and Narramore, and Cosgrove and Mallory hold similar views, as do many other Christian professionals.[17]

At the other extreme are persons like Hunt and McMahon, who argue in this manner:

[Psychology] is a pseudo-science riddled with contradiction and confusion. . . . The basic problem with the "all truth is God's truth" approach lies in the fact that psychology pretends to offer answers which, even if it were a science, it could never give. We have no quarrel with chemistry, medicine or physics, but with psychology's pretense to sci- entifically understand and deal with the heart of man, who is a spiritual being made in the image of God.[18]

A number of others, such as Adams, the Bobgans, and perhaps Kilpatrick, seem to agree with Hunt and McMahon's view.[19] These authors believe that psychology has little or nothing to offer; in fact, they view psychology as distinctly harmful.

A third group of Christians holds an intermediate position, seeing some value in psychology, but contending that biblical and psychological truth do not stand on equal footing. To them psychology must be made subject to Scripture. Advocates of such a view include McQuilkin and Crabb.[20]

In light of the diversity of views among Christians about the relationship between psychology and theology, it is understand- able that there is also a diversity of approaches to the problem of mental illness or psychopathology among pastors and Christian professionals. In general, two basic approaches have been taken. The first is one which largely adopts one of the many psychologi- cal theories, adapting it in various ways to fit the author's under- standing of Scripture. Proponents of the "all truth is God's truth" perspective generally take this approach.

In contrast are those who reject psychology on the grounds that it is anti-Christian. Instead they advocate "Christian Coun- seling" or "Biblical Counseling." Adherents of this view gener- ally reject the medical, sociopsychological, and systems models of mental illness; in their place they propose a moral or sin model. In Adams's words,

. . . the Scriptures plainly speak of both organically based problems as well as those problems that stem from sinful attitudes and behavior; but where, in all of God's Word, is there so much as a trace of any third source of problems which might approximate the modern concept of "mental illness."[21]

For Adams all problems come from sin. The solution is nouthetic counseling, an approach which confronts the individual with scriptural teaching about the sinful patterns in his or her life, counsels confession and repentance, and emphasizes change into conformity with God's Word. Adams advocates that all Christians take this approach, but he is especially concerned with those who are involved in pastoral ministry. In his view, this approach should be adequate for all mental-health problems except those rare instances which clearly have an organic (or biological) basis.

Since Jennifer's problems have no identified organic basis, adherents of this view would likely focus on exhorting her to acknowledge her present sinful conduct, repent, and change her ways. In the likely event that she proved unwilling or unable to admit her sin and repent, they would have little more to offer her until she was ready to do so.

Although proponents of the biblical and Christian counseling approaches often vehemently reject psychology, they seem to overlook the fact that in adopting counseling they are embracing techniques which have their intellectual roots in psychology and education. Those who have studied counseling theory readily recognize that familiar psychological models and theories underlie the popular "Christian counseling" and "biblical counseling" approaches.

For example, Jay Adams draws heavily on the writing of psychologist O. Hobart Mowrer; Lawrence Crabb's approach leans heavily on the rational emotive therapy of psychologist Albert Ellis; and William T. Kirwan extensively uses the ideas of the late humanistic psychologist, Carl Rogers.[22]

Advocates of these approaches are a minority. Most efforts to develop a Christian model acknowledge at least some aspects of the medical model. Further, the medical model enjoys widespread acceptance among respected professionals across the boundaries of a variety of mental-health disciplines, including psychiatry, psychology, and social work.

Any credible effort to deal with the complex issues involved in mental disorders must take into account the diversity of phenomena involved. Mark Cosgrove and James Mallory, in their book *Mental Health: A Christian Approach* provide one example of a successful attempt to deal with this complexity.[23] One of the major reasons for the continued diversity of models of mental disorders stems from this complexity and from the fact that so far no single model seems to adequately address the roles of physical, social, psychological, and spiritual issues involved. This will become clearer as we examine in more detail the scope of disorders included in DSM-III-R.

SUMMARY

Several models have been proposed over the years to account for the phenomenon now known as mental illness, including the spiritual model, the moral model, the medical model, the sociopsychological model, and the systems model. By far the most common model is the medical model. Some Christian theorists reject the medical model, and tend to reject the notion of mental illness entirely except for instances of organically caused difficulties, which are presumed to be rare.

If we are to understand the relationship of demonic influence to mental illness it is important that we understand the medical model, especially as incorporated in the DSM-III-R diagnostic system. It is to this issue that we turn in the next chapter.

CHAPTER SIX

MENTAL DISORDERS

While there are a number of views on the nature of mental illness, the standard reference of mental disorders in the United States, as we have said, is the American Psychiatric Association's *Diagnostic and Statistical Manual of Mental Disorders,* Third Edition, Revised (DSM-III-R).[1]

This chapter will examine the basic sections of DSM-III-R, including an overview of the major diagnostic categories and a consideration of the model of man which is implicit in the diagnostic system. The DSM-III-R diagnostic system encompasses three major classes of disorders in terms of cause or etiology.

First, there are many conditions which are clearly caused by physical diseases, such as tumors and strokes. Some of these are presumably outside the victim's control. Others, such as brain damage resulting from the abuse of alcohol or other controlled substances, are believed to be the result of the person's own actions.

Second are disorders or conditions known or strongly suspected to involve a biological predisposition, such as manic-depressive disorder and various forms of schizophrenia. However, it is believed that the person must be exposed to other factors, such as personal traumas and stressors, in order to develop the disorder.

Third are conditions in which no known or presumed biological factors are involved. These are often called functional disorders. For many of them, which include anxiety and depression, the person is presumed to have little or no personal responsibility in developing the disorder. However, for others of these disorders, personal actions, such as choosing to drink alcoholic beverages or to use a variety of legal or illegal drugs (but without resulting brain damage), may play an important role; examples include alcohol- and substance-abuse disorders (which may occur with prescribed medications as well as street drugs). Initially, we might conclude that these conditions result from sin, but as we shall see, often that is too simplistic an explanation.

If we are to understand the relationship between mental disorders and demonic influence, a basic grasp of the DSM-III-R diagnostic system is of great value. Those who are already familiar with DSM-III-R may wish to skim quickly over this chapter. All of us should remember, however, that mental disorders rarely have simple causes.

MULTIDIMENSIONAL DIAGNOSIS

With the publication of DSM-III-R, the diagnostic system adopted a procedure in which each person was to be evaluated on five different dimensions, or "axes," each of which involves a different type of information. The first three of these dimensions constitute the official diagnosis, and include 1) mental disorders, 2) developmental and personality disorders, and 3) physical disorders and conditions. The remaining dimensions include 4) severity of psychosocial stressors and 5) overall assessment of functioning during the past year; the last two are used primarily in treatment planning and in predicting outcome.

> [The first two dimensions] comprise the entire classification of mental disorders. . . . This separation ensures that consideration is given to the possible presence of disorders that are frequently overlooked when attention is directed to the usually more [obvious disorders of the first dimension].[2]

Obviously, an adequate evaluation of an individual's functioning requires taking into account information from each of these areas. The result is a complex and rather sophisticated system that seeks to encompass the complexity of human functioning.

Clinical Syndromes

The first dimension includes the clinical syndromes such as anxiety, depression and organically induced mental disorders. It is common for individuals to receive a diagnosis on both the first and second dimensions. In such instances, the diagnosis on the first dimension is assumed to be the principal diagnosis which is the focus for treatment unless it is specifically noted that the diagnosis on the second dimension is primary.

Jennifer, whom we discussed previously, would be classified under the clinical syndromes as a Multiple Personality Disorder. This mental disorder has no known or presumed biological cause, and it is unclear whether personal responsibility plays an important role in this condition.

Personality Disorders and Specific Developmental Disorders

The Personality Disorders, such as Paranoid Personality and Obsessive-Compulsive Personality, and specific developmental disorders, such as Mental Retardation and Dyslexia, are diagnosed on the second dimension. Everyone is presumed, from time to time, to show the personality patterns listed here to some degree or other. However, some individuals show these patterns in much more exaggerated and pervasive forms. Often the

Personality and Developmental Disorders result in considerable difficulty in personal-social functioning. Furthermore, some believe that these enduring patterns of responding to people and situations, when present in their more extreme forms, underly many of the mental disorders which are considered on the first dimension. When the person shows such an enduring pattern of disturbance in personality functioning or development, it is diagnosed in addition to, or instead of, clinical syndromes according to DSM-III-R. Also, this dimension "can be used to indicate specific personality traits when no Personality Disorder exists."[3]

A significant source of problems involves difficulty with school adjustment. These problems are categorized as Specific Developmental Disorders, and include reading, arithmetic, articulation, mixed and atypical categories.

Initially it might seem that the Specific Developmental Disorders are not mental disorders. However, there is a strong association between learning disorders, as these are often called, and mental health problems. Data suggests that as many as 80 percent of adolescents receiving hospitalized mental health treatment for substance abuse also show learning disabilities.[4] While one cannot safely conclude that learning disorders produce substance abuse, it seems likely that learning disorders are one of the contributing factors.

Physical Disorders and Conditions

As suggested above, it is recognized in DSM-III-R that mental disorders may produce or exacerbate physical conditions such as duodenal ulcers or high blood pressure. It is also recognized that physical conditions, such as hormonal imbalances, a stroke, or AIDS infections, may contribute to mental disorders. Assessment of physical disorders and conditions prompts the examiner to consider this dimension of the person, and to evaluate the interplay between mental and physical functioning; special emphasis is placed on the role of physical factors in the development and treatment of mental disorders.

Severity of Psychosocial Stressors

This dimension requires the examiner to explicitly assess the person's history of stressors in the past year and consider the role of such historical factors in the presenting complaint. It is believed that stressors may play a role in the development of a mental disorder, in worsening an existing mental disorder, or in recurrence of a former disorder.

The adjustment disorders in particular take into account the level of stress to which the individual has recently been exposed, and are defined in terms of harmful or inappropriate reaction to actual stress experienced in the past three months. Things to be considered as stressors include such experiences as moves, job loss, accident or injury, engagement or marriage, marital conflict or divorce, death, major financial changes, civil or criminal charges, and a host of other events. Stressors are rated on a scale from 1 (none) to 6 (catastrophic). Examples of catastrophic stressors include death of a child or spouse, and being taken as a hostage or placed in a concentration camp.

One example of a factor that might be coded here is the distress caused by the diagnosis of AIDS. In the *Surgeon General's Report on AIDS* it is noted that significant mental-health problems may result from receiving a diagnosis of AIDS:

> Upon being informed of infection with the AIDS virus, a young, active, vigorous person faces anxiety and depression brought on by fears associated with social isolation, illness and dying. Dealing with these individual and family concerns will require the best efforts of mental health professionals.[5]

One of the greatest concerns about widespread testing for AIDS is that a significant number of individuals will be falsely identified as AIDS carriers. Even with an error rate of one in a thousand, if 50 million are tested, 50 thousand will be falsely found to be carriers. The potential mental anguish of this is one of the major dilemmas which must be faced in deciding how to approach the AIDS problem.[6]

Global Assessment of Functioning

The Global (or overall) Assessment of Functioning (GAF) evaluation involves making a judgment about the individual's overall level of mental health, currently, and during the past year.

Ratings of current functioning will generally reflect the current need for treatment or care. Ratings of highest level of functioning during the past year frequently will have prognostic significance, because usually a person returns to his or her previous level of functioning after an episode of illness.[7]

In some disorders, such as schizophrenia, a defining criterion is deterioration from a previous level of functioning. Assessment of adaptive functioning for the past year requires the examiner to explicitly evaluate social relationships, occupational functioning, and use of leisure time. Ratings of past and current functioning are made on a scale from 1 (persistent danger to self or others or inability to maintain minimal personal hygiene) to 90 (good functioning in all areas with symptoms absent or minimal).

OVERVIEW OF MENTAL DISORDERS

Table 1 presents a brief overview of the DSM-III-R diagnostic system. Particular attention should be given to the causes or etiology of the various mental disorders as well as to gaining an overview of the kinds of symptoms typical in each major diagnostic group. Though somewhat complex, this information will be important to later discussions of the relationship between mental illness and the demonic.

As a foundational principle, in constructing DSM-III-R it was decided that priority would be given to diagnosing an organic mental disorder over functional disorders whenever the symptoms fit with an organic disorder and signs of organic dysfunction or historical factors supporting an organic diagnosis are present. Organic disorders are those of physical origin; functional disorders, though often similar in symptoms, have no known physical causes. Thus diagnosis of organic depression takes precedence over diagnosis of major depression as a functional mood disorder.

Mental Disorders in DSM-III-R*

I. Clinical Syndromes

  A. Disorders usually first evident in infancy, childhood or adolescence
    1. Disruptive-behavior disorders
    2. Anxiety disorders of childhood or adolescence
    3. Eating disorders
    4. Gender-identity disorders
    5. Tic disorders
    6. Elimination disorders
    7. Speech disorders not elsewhere classified
    8. Other disorders of infancy, childhood, or adolescence

  B. Organic mental disorders
    1. Dementias arising before and during old age
    2. Psychoactive substance-induced organic mental disorders (e.g., organic disorders due to alcohol or narcotic dependence)
    3. Organic mental disorders associated with physical disorders or conditions, or for which the cause is unknown

  C. Psychoactive substance-use disorders (e.g., nonorganic disorders due to alcohol or narcotic dependence)

  D. Schizophrenia

  E. Delusional (paranoid) disorder

  F. Psychotic disorders not elsewhere classified

  G. Mood disorders
    1. Bipolar (manic-depressive) disorders
    2. Depressive disorders

  H. Anxiety disorders

  I. Somatoform disorders (physical disorders without organic causes)

  J. Dissociative disorders (e.g., Multiple Personality Disorder)

  K. Sexual disorders

  L. Sleep disorders

  M. Factitious (faked) disorders

  N. Impulse-control disorders not elsewhere classified

  O. Adjustment disorders

  P. Psychological factors affecting physical condition

II. Developmental Disorders and Personality Disorders

  A. Developmental Disorders (usually first seen in childhood)
    1. Mental retardation
    2. Pervasive developmental disorders (e.g., infantile autism)
    3. Specific developmental disorders (e.g., dyslexia)
    4. Other developmental disorders

  B. Personality Disorders

III. Physical Disorders and Conditions

IV. Severity of Psychosocial Stressors

V. Overall Assessment of Functioning

Table 1

*Adapted from American Psychiatric Association's Diagnostic and Statistical Manual of Mental Disorders, Third Edition, Revised (DSM – III – R).

A second foundational principle is to give priority to diagnosis of more pervasive disorders, even though symptoms associated with a more specific or "isolated" disorder also are observed. For example, if schizophrenic symptoms are present along with chronic mild depression, technically known as dysthymic disorder, schizophrenia is diagnosed since chronic mild depression often accompanies schizophrenia.

In the next section we will examine several mental disorders in DSM-III-R to illustrate the interactions among biological, psychological, social, and spiritual factors in mental disorders.

EXAMPLES OF MENTAL DISORDERS

Mental Retardation

One of the most prominent classes of disorders among children is mental retardation. This disorder involves general intellectual functioning which is significantly below average, associated with or resulting in deficits or impairments in adaptive behavior beginning before age eighteen. Low intelligence test scores and inability to live independently and meet the normal social responsibilities expected of the child's age and cultural group are the primary criteria.

Causes "may be primarily biological, psychosocial, or an interaction of both."[8] Numerous biological causes of retardation have been discovered. Among these are Down's Syndrome or Trisomy-21, Tay-Sachs disease, phenylketonuria, cretinism, hydrocephaly, and severe shortage of oxygen during the birth process. In general, mental retardation stemming from biological causes is moderate to profound, thus diagnosis generally occurs at birth or in the first few months of life.

About 75 percent of the cases of retardation are only mildly severe. In the majority of these, no clear biological factor can be identified, though biological causes cannot confidently be ruled out. Mild retardation is believed to result from one or more of three factors: 1) genetic causes; 2) environmentally influenced biological factors, such as malnutrition and lead poisoning; 3) psychosocial causes, such as relatively deprived early-childhood environment and learning experiences.

Conduct Disorders and Oppositional Defiant Disorder

Conduct Disorders are defined as a "persistent pattern of conduct in which the basic rights of others and major age-appropriate societal norms or rules are violated."[9] The conduct is more serious than the ordinary mischief and pranks of children and adolescents; it includes stealing, aggression, lying, cheating, truancy, property destruction—such as setting fires—rape, extortion, mugging and other such things.

Conduct Disorders are divided into two types, depending on whether the person engages in such activities alone (solitary) or with others (group). There is little firm evidence that biological factors play a role in these disorders, though it is known that such difficulties tend to run in families.

The Oppositional Defiant Disorder lacks the serious violation of the rights of others found in the Conduct Disorders, but includes acts of defiance, negativism, and hostility directed primarily toward parents and other adult authority figures. Denial is common; the person justifies the conduct and does not view himself or herself as acting inappropriately. Temper, moodiness, and the use of drugs, alcohol, and tobacco are common in this condition.

In conduct and oppositional disorders, biological factors are presumed to play at most a minor role. The primary causes are generally presumed to be psychological and socioemotional. Spiritual factors may also be important in these disorders. They may reflect overt sinful conduct. Also, there is the possibility that some of these patterns of behavior could be due to demonic influence.

Organic Mental Disorders (Axis I)

Organic Mental Disorders involve a known or presumed biological cause that can be demonstrated from a review of the individual's history, physical examination, or laboratory testing. For Organic Mental Disorders there should be a corresponding diagnosis of a physical disorder or condition. Physical brain disorder is the primary diagnosis, while the mental-disorder diagnosis describes the way in which the brain injury manifests itself in mental/psychological functioning. "The essential feature of all these disorders is a psychological or behavioral abnormality associated with transient or permanent dysfunction of the brain."[10]

Organic Mental Disorders may result from a host of biological causes, including the effects of aging, toxic effects of prescription drugs, alcohol or substance abuse, brain tumors, strokes and hardening of cerebral arteries, brain injuries, infections, and nutritional deficiencies or excesses. The symptomatic manifestations are quite diverse, including such features as delirium, delusions, hallucinations, impaired judgment, dementia, amnesia, apathy, lethargy, incontinence, psychomotor impairment, anxiety, and depression.

A recent addition to organic mental disorders is dementia due to the AIDS virus. In the *Surgeon General's Report on AIDS* it is noted that "mental disease (dementia) will occur in some patients who have the AIDS virus before they have any other manifestation such as ARC or classic AIDS."[11] A recent newsletter for mental-health professionals elaborates:

> Recently it has become apparent that, in addition to psychological reactions and organic brain conditions resulting from opportunistic infections, some people with AIDS show symptoms of other types of neurological damage. HTLV-III directly infects some cells in the brain. . . . central nervous system involvement may be extensive in some patients. Some symptoms that appear to be psychologically caused may in fact be organic in origin and degenerative in course.[12]

It is clear that the immediate cause of the Organic Mental Disorders involves some malfunction of the brain. However, even in these disorders, personal responsibility may play a significant role. For example, personal choices regarding life style and behavior are involved in the substance use or abuse which results in certain organic disorders; similarly, the personal choice to engage in promiscuous sexual activity may result in contracting AIDS. In other instances, the action of persons other than the patient/client is involved, for example, when head injuries are the result of assault and abuse. In still other instances, such as disorders caused by aging or infections, no personal responsibility seems to be involved. These three patterns correspond to personal sin, the sin of others, and sin in the world. Finally, some believe that patterns of conduct which lead to organic mental disorders, such as substance abuse, may be the result of demonic influence.

Mood Disorders

Mood refers to a prolonged emotional condition that colors all the person's mental life. It may be predominantly depressive or elated, or these two may alternate in a cyclic pattern. In their fully-developed form, both elated and depressed mood may be associated with disturbances in thinking and loss of reality contact, but the mood disturbance occurs first and is presumed to be primary.

Ahmed   Ahmed came to a large East-coast city, took the largest suite of rooms in the most expensive hotel, and presented himself as a prince from a rich, Middle-East oil kingdom. He brought an entourage of several other guests who took nearby suites, all on his tab. They invited a number of prominent people from the town, and began a party which went on for several days. As the bill mounted, the hotel manager became uneasy and requested payment. Soon he discovered that Ahmed was an impostor, that he had no money, and thus could not pay the bill. Charges were pressed, and Ahmed was arrested. At the arraignment his attorney claimed that Ahmed was unaware of what he was doing, and thus could not be held responsible due to insanity; Ahmed was experiencing a manic disorder (a clinical syndrome diagnosed on the first dimension).

Obsessive Compulsive Disorders

Obsessive Disorders are recurrent thoughts, ideas, images or impulses that the person professes not to desire and finds repugnant, yet reports he or she is unable to resist. Compulsions are repetitive behavioral rituals performed to produce or prevent some event or situation; however, the person recognizes that the activity has no relationship to the event or is clearly excessive.

Leila   Leila was a mild-mannered woman in her late fifties.

She came to me on referral from another counselor for help with a compulsive pattern of washing herself. When I first saw her our appointments were at 6:00 P.M. In order to be ready on time, Leila rose at 5:30 A.M. to begin her shower and get dressed. She spent all day washing and rinsing her body, inch by inch. Yet she could not complete the task and make it to our appointment on time.

A recent convert to a charismatic faith, Leila struggled with the belief that her problem was the result of sin, or of demonic influence. She prayed for deliverance, and attended healing meetings in which others prayed for her; yet she experienced no change.

My goal in working with her was to change the habit patterns that made up her washing ritual. We worked on using the soap to lather up only once during each washing; on dressing herself completely after washing rather than washing after donning each article of clothing; on shutting off the water and beginning the next task, rather than washing again when she touched the faucet due to fear that she was now contaminated.

Leila was obsessive-compulsive. There were spiritual dimensions to her problem as well, involving reluctance to carry out some aspects of her wifely duties in the home, resentment toward her husband, and ingratitude toward God for allowing her to experience this difficulty. These were addressed, along with a focus on practical behavior changes.

Leila found it hard to accept the view that her problem was partly psychological, not merely spiritual; so long as she viewed it as spiritual she believed that all she could do was pray and believe that God would heal her. This made it easy for her to justify doing nothing herself. I encouraged her to pray and believe, but also to work as God enabled her, to promote the healing process through her own diligent efforts. As she did so she gradually made progress.

Somatoform Disorders

The main features of this group of disorders are physical symptoms suggesting physical disorders (hence, somatoform) for which there are no positive medical or laboratory findings. The physical symptoms are a response to psychological stress or personal and interpersonal conflict rather than to real physical trauma or disease.[13]

Somatoform Disorders may take the form of preoccupation with an imagined physical defect. Or they may manifest themselves in an exaggerated concern over minor imperfections in bodily appearance, general physical complaints involving one or more of the major organ systems (such as gastrointestinal complaints or heart palpitations), loss or alteration in physical functioning (such as weakness in the arms or chronic pain in the absence of any adequate physical explanation), or exaggerated complaint about normal aches and pains.

While superficially similar to some aspects of demonic influence, in most instances it seems likely that Somatoform Disorders are physical reactions to psychological distress. They illustrate the interaction of psychological and physical functioning.

Dissociative Disorders

The central element in Dissociative Disorders is loss of personal identity and integration which is not due to organic brain syndromes. Disturbances may occur in identity, consciousness, or motor behavior, though disturbance in motor behavior must be accompanied by disturbed consciousness to fit this disorder.

Multiple Personality is a Dissociative Disorder which involves the presence of distinct personalities or personality states which alternate in the dominant role, usually suddenly, and with distinct personality patterns associated with each.

> The **belief that one is possessed** by another person, spirit or entity may occur as a symptom of Multiple Personality Disorder. In such cases the complaint of being "possessed" is actually the experience of the alternate personality's influence on the person's behavior and mood. However, the feeling that one is "possessed" may also be a delusion in a psychotic disorder, such as Schizophrenia, not a symptom of a Dissociative Disorder [emphasis in the original].[14]

The popular accounts, *The Three Faces of Eve*, and *Sybil* are based on Multiple Personality Disorders.[15] Jennifer, described in chapter 5, is an example of multiple personality. Multiple personality is the mental disorder that most closely resembles demonic possession. As we shall see later, some believe that demon possession sometimes occurs in persons with multiple personality.

Sexual Disorders

Sexual disorders involve a wide variety of disturbances in which psychological factors are the presumed cause. Disorders of sexual functioning for which the cause is physiological are not included in DSM-III-R.

Early editions of DSM-II included homosexuality as a specific mental disorder. In later editions it was deleted, although the context clearly implied homosexuality was a mental disorder (a footnote reveals that a vote of the American Psychiatric Association resulted in this change). A later section of this chapter addresses homosexuality in some detail.

Factitious Disorders

In Factitious Disorders, physiological or psychological symptoms are intentionally produced or feigned by the individual. There is a compulsive quality about these acts which suggests that they are deliberate and purposive, but the individual uses them toward ends which he or she is unlikely to consciously choose. When physical symptoms are present they may seem so real that the person has repeated hospitalizations for medical care.

Factitious Disorders may mimic either psychological or physical illnesses. Examples of factitious disorders include complaints of dementia, psychosis, false pregnancies, dizziness, rashes, or abdominal complaints. Virtually any form of physical or psychological complaint may occur with this disorder. It usually is recognized and diagnosed because of the extreme frequency of complaints, the absence of tissue pathology, and/or the inconsistency of symptoms.

Emily Emily saw her enterologist repeatedly with complaints of uncontrollable diarrhea. Although repeated on several occasions, all of the diagnostic tests yielded negative results. Subsequently, it was discovered that she was obsessed with maintaining her weight below 106 pounds. Anytime it exceeded this level she took large doses of laxatives to purge herself of the food which she had consumed and thus reduce her weight. The laxatives accounted for the diarrhea. Emily's disorder is classified as factitious, though not all Factitious Disorders involve physical symptoms.

Whether or not we consider excessive use of laxatives sinful, Emily clearly was responsible for producing her own problems. Moreover, she misled her doctor regarding how the symptoms came about, though it is not clear whether she herself was aware of the relationship between her habits and the symptoms. Some might consider Emily to be under demonic influence. Certainly, she had made maintaining her 106-pound figure a false god to which she paid repeated homage.

Psychological Factors Affecting Physical Condition (Axis I)

This classification is used where psychological factors cause a physical illness or make it significantly worse. Judgment is involved, but this can often be easily recognized when physical symptoms repeatedly begin with or become more severe following identifiable psychological stressors. In the past these have often been called psychosomatic or psychophysiological disorders. Headaches which occur following interpersonal conflict fit this classification. Other examples include lower back pain, migraine and tension headaches, duodenal ulcers, ulcerative colitis, and many others.

All of us have heard the expressions: "She's a pain in the neck." "He's a hothead." "You make me sick." These statements reflect the fact that our minds and bodies interact. While the spiritual dimension of this class of mental disorders is often ignored, McMillen, in his book *None of These Diseases* makes a strong case for the conclusion that many physical and mental disorders involve spiritual issues such as unforgiveness, bitterness, hatred, and worry.[16]

ISSUES FROM A CHRISTIAN PERSPECTIVE

As was shown in the foregoing discussion, the DSM-III-R diagnostic system is complex and multifaceted. It attempts to account for all of the complexity of mental disorders as they are currently viewed by practitioners from a variety of disciplines and theoretical perspectives. It includes three major classes of disorders in terms of cause or etiology: genetic and biological factors, psychological factors, and personal-social factors.

Because humans are complex beings in whom biological, psychological, and personal-social aspects are in continuous interplay, these factors interact in a variety of complex ways in producing mental disorders. For example, there is evidence that at least in some instances involvement in substance abuse is as much the result of mental disorders as the cause of them; many individuals use alcohol or drugs as a form of self-medication for depression, anxiety and other mental disorders.[17] There is even one passage in Proverbs that appears to support this practice (see Proverbs 31:4–7).

Further, while the initial decision to consume alcohol or to use drugs is presumably voluntary, once the process has begun there is strong evidence that the probability of that person's becoming a problem drinker or drug abuser is significantly influenced by biological factors which are presumed to be genetic.[18]

The Role of Sin

Sin in the World By this point it should be quite clear that one cannot responsibly dismiss all of the mental disorders included in DSM-III-R by saying with Adams that the problem is sin.[19] At least not if one means *personal* sin.

Yet, in another sense the problem is indeed sin. First, the presence of sin in our world as the result of the Fall, and the resulting distortion of the whole created order, caused death in its many-faceted forms to be passed to all men (Rom. 5:10–21). Without sin in the world there would be neither physical nor mental illness. Moreover, in the world to come these will be abolished (Rev. 21:1–4). Thus, *in the sense that all evil is the result of sin in the world, mental disorders are the result of sin;* but mental disorders are not necessarily the result of the sufferer's personal sin. Mental disorders may be the result of sin in the world, the sin of others, and/or personal sin.

Personal Sin As we have already seen, personal-social life style is sometimes a major factor in mental illness. Thus it seems true that *at least in some instances mental illness is the result of personal sin.*

The Sin of Others There is another possibility as well. *In some instances, mental illness is the result of being sinned against.* The child who is brutally beaten by an unloving parent with the result that serious brain damage is sustained, the chronic depressive who was the victim of repeated psychological and sexual abuse, the car-accident victim who was hit by a drunk driver: these are the victims of the sinfulness of others.

Often it is not possible to distinguish among sin in the world, personal sin, and the sinfulness of others as influences in a given mental disorder unless the person's history is well-known. For example, organic brain syndromes can be produced by a vicious assault or by completely accidental injuries.

The presence of brain damage may go undetected for years if the effects are mild to moderate, or develop gradually. Senile dementia may illustrate such a pattern in which repeated minor strokes or coronary blood clots produce brain atrophy and progressive loss of functioning which may not be detectable by current medical techniques, or which may only recently be detectable by the development of sophisticated procedures (such as positron emissions tomography and magnetic resonance imagery).

It is important to remember that the simple fact that no medical problems are diagnosed does not satisfactorily rule out physical causes (the effects of sin in the world) as the basis of a given mental disorder. Our knowledge in these areas is, unfortunately, still very limited. Medical diagnosis is subject both to limited knowledge and human fallibility.

Another example of this confusion between physical and psychological sources of mental disorders occurs in the area of "irritable bowel syndrome," a condition that fits under the classification, "Somatization Disorder"; presumably the disorder is a result of anxiety or "nerves." Recent research has shown that a number of medical disorders can produce an "irritable bowel." Previously, due to inadequate knowledge and diagnostic capabilities, persons with these diseases were diagnosed as having Somatization Disorders. Among the causes of misdiagnosed gastrointestinal disorders are food allergies, such as allergic reactions to milk (galactosemia, or lactose intolerance), reactions to gluten and cane sugar, and a parasitic infection of the digestive tract known as ghiardiasis. Also, gastrointestinal complaints sometimes develop as side effects of necessary medications.[20]

Spiritual Well-Being

There is much in Scripture to suggest that a healthy relationship with God should result in better mental health and physical well-being.[21] In the past few years a body of literature has begun to develop which points to this precise conclusion from a scientific perspective as well. Psychologists Craig Ellison and Raymond Paloutzian developed the Spiritual Well-Being Scale as an index of spiritual health. Research with this scale indicates that spiritual well-being is positively correlated with many indicators of physical and psychological health, such as self-esteem, satisfaction with family life, and sociopsychological adjustment to seminary. Similarly, spiritual well-being has been found to be negatively related to many indicators of physical or psychological difficulties such as depression, loneliness, aggressiveness, elevated blood pressure, complaints of chronic pain, and being overweight.[22]

With the goal of making assessment more complete, and in light of the findings on spiritual well-being, perhaps we should consider adding an additional dimension to the DSM-III-R coding, thus providing for evaluation from a Christian perspective. This dimension would assess spiritual condition. It could address such questions as whether the person professes any religious faith, importance of religion to the individual, frequency of church attendance, frequency of personal devotionals, and any recent changes in the person's religious life. Use of the Spiritual Well-Being Scale or some similar instrument might also be helpful.

Even with provision for assessing the person's spiritual condition, the use of the DSM-III-R diagnostic system, or any similar classification scheme, poses unique problems from a Christian perspective. Recognition of this does not mean that we should reject the diagnostic system; indeed, to do so would likely create more problems than it would solve. However, the added spiritual dimension must be accounted for in some fashion. Another major problem we must address involves the relationship of demonic influence to this classificatory system; further discussion of this issue is presented later.

HOMOSEXUALITY

The place of homosexuality in the *Diagnostic and Statistical Manual* illustrates some of the complexity of the diagnostic classification system. As noted earlier, in the first two editions of the manual, homosexuality per se was viewed as a mental disorder. However, in 1969, in a controversial decision, the American Psychiatric Association voted to remove it as a mental disorder. For a time the section on homosexuality was replaced with a new category, that of "Sexual Orientation Disturbance [Homosexuality]":

This is for individuals whose sexual interests are directed primarily toward people of the same sex and who are either disturbed by, in conflict with, or wish to change their sexual orientation. This classification is distinguished from homosexuality, which by itself does not constitute a psychiatric disorder. Homosexuality *per se* is one form of sexual behavior, and with other forms of sexual behavior which are not by themselves psychiatric disorders, is not listed in this nomenclature.[23]

This new category was merely inserted in context following the introduction to sexual deviations which defined sexual deviation:

[such are] sexual interests [which] are directed primarily toward objects other than people of the opposite sex, toward sexual acts not usually associated with coitus, or toward coitus performed under bizarre circumstances as in necrophilia, pedophilia, sexual sadism, and fetishism.[24]

This definition of sexual deviations clearly implies homosexuality to be abnormal. A footnote was appended, acknowledging the inconsistency.

Some have argued that this change in the diagnostic system was basically a political act. They believed that homosexuals had effectively lobbied to have themselves declared normal. It is rumored that at least one person charged that the voting on this decision was rigged. Regardless of the merits of this allegation, it is clear that there are diverse views about both the morality and the psychological status of homosexuality.

Although homosexuality is perhaps one of the more obvious examples, there is controversy about a number of the other categories included in the diagnostic system as well. That controversy, in part, resulted in the recent publication of DSM-III-R. Even so, disagreements remain; controversy about the revisions in DSM-III-R had made the news even before it went to press.[25]

The diagnostic system involves values, and bears evidence of disagreement about those values. Many are inclined to view mental disorders as categorically distinct from medical disorders. However, it is not wise to make too much of that distinction. Medical diagnosis is also based on values, most specifically the value that it is good to be well and bad to be ill or injured, and worse yet to die. One feature that distinguishes physical medicine is that there tends to be greater agreement about its values.[25] But even they are not universal, as is demonstrated by the fact that civil suits try to decide whether a child should receive surgery despite the objections of parents who are Christian Science practitioners. Similar value controversies arise over other medical and bioethical matters. In these instances the dispute is sometimes over the fact of illness; equally often it is over the wisdom of treatment even when the presence of illness or injury is undisputed.

Because of the controversy regarding homosexuality, further comments about a Christian view of homosexuality may help to illustrate some of the issues raised here.

First, in a recent review, John Money shows that disturbances in hormonal levels prenatally and shortly after birth may result in internal genital organs, external genital organs, or both internal and external organs which are inconsistent with the sex chromosomes at a genetic level. Thus, at a biological level it is possible for both masculine and feminine characteristics to coexist in a single organism, and to do so in a variety of ways. Fortunately, such anomalies are relatively infrequent.[26]

In addition to anomalies of physical structure, discrepancies may also occur between sexual structure and sexual behavior patterns. A variety of discordant behavioral patterns may be fostered by abnormalities at the biological level. These include behavioral tendencies toward homosexuality and bisexuality.

The steroid hormones such as prednisone and medrol are examples of commonly prescribed medications which can affect sexual development. It seems likely that exposure to steroids during crucial developmental periods may dramatically alter external genitalia and/or the brain-controlled predispositions influencing sexual behavior. However, it is doubtful that this factor, by itself, accounts for the current level of homosexuality. Homosexuality is a complex issue at both the biological and social levels.

In addressing the religious/moral aspects of sexuality, several things need to be acknowledged at the outset. First, God made humans as sexual persons, and pronounced that sex within the God-given limits of marriage is "holy and undefiled" (see Hebrews 13:4; cp. 1 Cor. 7:1–4).

Second, God set explicit limits on the overt expression of sexuality. Homosexuality, fornication, adultery, bestiality, and a wide variety of other sexual behaviors are clearly prohibited by Scripture (Exod. 20:14; Lev. 20:10–23; 1 Cor. 5:1–7; 6:15–19).

Third, God calls us to forsake sexual lust, the tendency to dwell on and be preoccupied with sexual thoughts and fantasies (Matt. 5:27–32). It is important to distinguish between being attracted to or "falling in love" with members of the same sex and being overtly involved in sexual intimacies. It appears that it is at this point that the role of sexual socialization becomes vital in a person's conforming to the God-given standards for sexual conduct. Although some persons are biologically predisposed to be attracted to other persons of the same sex, they can learn to control their impulses, thus conforming to godly standards; these same principles apply to those attracted to members of the opposite sex to whom they are not married (1 Cor. 6:9–11).

In light of the findings of Money and his colleagues it appears that some people, at least without the benefit of modern surgery, fail to develop complete external genitalia, and thus may be incapable of heterosexual intercourse; perhaps these are those whom the Bible describes as "eunuchs who were born that way." Others may have their sexual organs altered by men, often for cruel and inhumane reasons; these are "eunuchs who were made eunuchs by men" (Matt. 19:12).

Finally, some may find themselves, by reason of hormonal or social influences, attracted to members of the same sex. In order to live a godly life, these may find it necessary to forsake sexual intimacy for the kingdom of God. This group, in most respects, is comparable to those with heterosexual interests who eschew marriage for the sake of God's kingdom (see 1 Corinthians 7:24–40).

As we have seen, some may find themselves attracted to members of the same sex for reasons over which they have little or no control. To the extent this is true, we must view this as the effect of sin in our world, or, in some instances, the effect of the sin of parents or influential others, but not of personal sin on the part of the individual. However, when the individual chooses to satisfy his or her sexual impulses outside of the marital relationship, the problem is sin whether the transgression is heterosexual or homosexual. It is to this matter that Scripture speaks. By contrast, DSM-III-R is concerned with all the psychological dimensions of sexual-identity problems whether or not they result in illegal or sinful acts, provided they are a source of concern to the individual.

In light of the above, for those charged with the care of troubled persons it is too simplistic to dismiss the problem of homosexuality with the simple statement that the problem is sin.

SUMMARY

In this chapter we have examined the diagnostic system for mental disorders in DSM-III-R. It is a complex system which takes into account biological, personal, and social factors that cause mental disorders, and considers a highly diverse set of symptomatic manifestations. Disorders are diagnosed on five dimensions, including mental disorders, personality disorders, physical disorders, severity of psychosocial stressors, and global assessment of functioning during the past year. In addition, it was suggested, a sixth dimension might be helpful to assess spiritual functioning, since the spiritual dimension presumably interacts with the physical and psychological dimensions.

Issues considered in diagnosis include the specific symptoms, their severity and duration, presumed causative factors, history of prior functioning, age of the individual, presence of other mental or physical disorders, and a number of other things. It was suggested that mental disorders are too complex to be dismissed as simply the result of personal sin, although personal sin, sin in the world, and the effects of the sin of others each may result in mental disorders. Finally, homosexuality was examined as an example of a disorder that involves a complex interaction among physical, social, and spiritual factors.

Mental disorders may be caused by genetic influences; they may be the result of accident, injury, disease, or exposure to substances on a voluntary or involuntary basis; they may result from clearly identified physiological malfunctions. Other mental disorders, many of which are attributed to psychological factors, are of unknown origins. Some disorders are associated with acts which are considered crimes in most states.

Value considerations are important in determining which behaviors will be labeled as mental disorders.[27] This is a well-recognized, if uncomfortable, aspect of mental disorders. The controversy over the insanity plea as a defense in criminal trials is one example of its practical implications. While Scripture is normative in establishing the nature and scope of sin, and for all true theology, it was not intended to define the limits of other disciplines, even those which most closely relate to its subject matter. For example, although the Bible contains a great deal of historical and geographical information, it is neither a history nor a geography text. In a similar manner, the Bible is not a diagnostic tool for mental disorders. DSM-III-R is designed to be just such a tool, however imperfect. While fault can be found with DSM-III-R from a number of perspectives, including a Christian one, we would do well to emulate mental-health professionals in using this system until a better one is developed to replace it. The diagnostic system simplifies communication among counselors, whether Christian or non-Christian, and among members of different professions, such as social workers, physicians, and counselors. Often, several persons need to communicate together about a single counselee, and the DSM-III-R system helps.

One of the thornier problems of the diagnostic system is the relationship of demonic influence to the various classifications. At first impression it might appear that there is no place for demonic influence. We shall turn to this issue in some detail in the next chapter.

CHAPTER SEVEN

DEMON POSSESSION

In chapter 3 we examined scriptural teachings about demons and demonic influence. Here we will focus specifically on the characteristic features of "demon possession" as manifested in Scripture, and in the writings of those involved in deliverance ministry. Next, we will consider the ways in which a person may come under demonic influence, here called avenues into the demonic. Then we will consider limitations of the biblical accounts of demon possession. Finally, we will examine demonic influence in other cultures.

CHARACTERISTICS OF DEMON POSSESSION

Because the English translations of the New Testament use the expression "demon possession," and because those involved

in deliverance ministries also typically refer to demon possession, we will use that expression in this section as we examine
the characteristic features of those who experience this extreme
form of demonic influence.

Dickason, quoting Unger, defines demon possession as "a
condition in which one or more evil spirits or demons inhabit
the body of a human being and can take complete control of
their victim at will."[1] Thus one aspect of demonic influence is
the loss of personal control over what one says and does, and
presumably over what one thinks and feels as well.

Although Dickason uses the expression "demonic possession,"
he repeatedly states that the issue is not one of ownership.

Again, the term *possessed* is misleading. . . . The real
concept is invasion and control to some degree, lesser or
greater; but never ownership.[2]

The demon . . . seeks to control whatever area of life or
whatever behavior is not controlled by the Holy Spirit. The
issue is still control, as the term *demonization* means [em-
phasis in original].[3]

At this point Dickason blurs an important distinction, that between unbeliever and believer. As noted earlier, the unbeliever
belongs to Satan; thus the demon-possessed unbeliever is both
owned and controlled by Satan. By contrast, the believer belongs to the kingdom of God, thus is not owned by Satan. Further, there is no biblical data to indicate that the believer can be
demon possessed.

Other aspects of demonic influence, in its extreme forms,
include loss of consciousness, speaking with another voice, and
projection of a distinct personality. Koch suggests that descriptions of demonic possession in Scripture indicate that it is
manifested by unusual physical strength, outbursts of rage,
disintegration of the personality, and supernatural sensibilities
such as clairvoyance and precognition.[4] In addition, we have
found scriptural accounts to include going about without clothing; inability to see, hear, or speak; and bizarre behavior (see
chapter 3).

Case studies reported by those involved in deliverance ministries suggest that characteristics of possessed persons include one or more of the following: moral depravity; melancholy; apparent idiocy; ecstatic episodes; extreme aggression; periods of unconsciousness; foaming at the mouth; resistance to a wide variety of religious activities such as prayer and Scripture reading; speaking in unlearned languages; phantom pain; depression; impure thoughts; obsession with or participation in actions of a sexual, sensual, and hostile nature; hearing "voices" that utter condemnatory statements or order acts such as murder or suicide; and suicidal obsessions.[5]

Many of the features observed in those believed to be demon possessed parallel characteristics found in scriptural examples. This is no great surprise, since those concerned with demon possession are usually professing Christians and, at least to some degree, scholars of Scripture. This makes it difficult to clearly conclude whether their observations and reports may be biased to some degree by what scriptural accounts have led them to expect. This concern is particularly significant since these accounts come almost exclusively from case studies rather than more rigorous scientific investigations with standardized procedures for observation, statistical analysis, and checks on the reliability of the resulting data.

Clearly, it is fairly easy for skeptics to dismiss accounts of possession as little more than naive credulity. This is particularly likely since many of those who profess to have dealt with demon possession seem to find demons everywhere; at the same time, those in deliverance ministries seem to have little notion of the human side of evil. However, we should not dismiss the notion of possession too quickly merely for these reasons. The biblical evidence is overwhelming that Jesus viewed persons as "possessed" and cast out demons from them. How then can we constructively address the criticisms of the skeptics while affirming that such phenomena do occur?

Table 2 presents a summary, taken from the writings of several authors, of the features observed in those "possessed."

Some thorny problems are raised by the list of characteristics in Table 2. First, it is difficult to distinguish many of the reported cases of demon possession from exaggerated forms of

---

> ### Characteristics of Demon Possession[5]
>
> Knowledge of supernatural
> Supernatural strength
> Going about naked
> Unable to hear, speak
> Seizures
> Blindness
> Use of "different" voice
> Presence of distinct personalities
> Bizarre behavior
> Fierce, violent behavior
> Unusual behavior/attitudes (e.g., vicious toward self)
> Feeling of overpowering evil
> Self-report of demonic influence
>
> ### Table 2

everyday patterns, most of which are sinful. Second, many presumably possessed persons do not manifest the features presented in this chart. Third, as we shall see in chapter 9, those with mental disorders as defined by DSM-III-R may also manifest many of the same characteristics found in those demon possessed.

Mack Mack exhibited an obsession with pornography and peep shows, together with chronic masturbation. In addition, he showed general disruption in his social relationships. He came for counseling when his wife discovered he had been buying pornographic magazines. She insisted that he get help. They had been to a spiritual counselor who suggested that Mack was possessed by a demon of lust; the counselor had attempted to cast out the demon, but to no avail. Ultimately, the counselor concluded, with some justification, that Mack did not sincerely desire to be delivered.

In counseling it was soon discovered that Mack's sexual habits traced to his childhood, when he was one of a group of boys who spent their time stealing pornographic magazines and engaging in a variety of sexual activities with each other and with anyone else available. This pattern of sexual obsession and promiscuous sexual activity had continued into adulthood, even after Mack's marriage. His wife had discovered only one aspect of this far more pervasive pattern.

At what point does one conclude that a person such as Mack is demonically influenced rather than merely exhibiting a chronic pattern of sinful behavior? Could Mack be both sinful and demonically influenced—even possessed?

In a similar fashion, it is believed that most people become discouraged at times, and many become depressed, at least on occasion. Suicidal and homicidal thoughts and actions are also commonplace. For example, it is reported that C. H. Spurgeon suffered from serious bouts of depression.[6] His condition appears to fit the criteria for a major depressive disorder as defined in DSM-III-R.[7]

The biblical accounts of Elijah and Jonah suggest that they, like Spurgeon, may have been depressed (see 1 Kings 19; Jon. 4). It seems likely that to some greater or lesser degree these men were demonically influenced, or at least that demonic forces attempted such influence. Perhaps some would say that they were possessed by the demon of depression, though it seems doubtful that they manifested the symptoms described in Table 2.

The mere presence of depressive, suicidal, or homicidal features is not enough, it seems, to warrant one to conclude that demonic influence is present to an extraordinary degree. What then is sufficient evidence?

If one examines the entire list of characteristics of demonic possession presented in Table 2, it appears that this list could be separated into two groupings: 1) patterns common in mental illness, and 2) common sinful patterns which are also found sometimes in mental illness (see Table 3). It appears that when we examine behavioral manifestations there is little unique to distinguish demon possession.

The manifestations of demonic influence can most readily be observed in those circumstances where demonic influence is most obvious. Thus it is helpful, at least initially, to focus on these more overt forms of demonic influence. Keep in mind, however, that demonic influence varies tremendously in terms of degree; different individuals may show many or few of the features described here. Similarly, these characteristics may be present to greater or lesser degrees, and for larger or smaller periods of time.

It is important that we not make the error of assuming, merely

> ### Characteristics of Demon Possession and Other Maladies[9]
>
> Features Associated with Mental Disorders
>   Unable to hear, speak
>   Seizures
>   Blindness
>   Use of "different" voice
>   Presence of distinct personality
>   Bizarre behavior
>   Unusual behavior/attitudes (e.g., vicious toward self)
>   Feeling of overpowering evil
>   Self-report of demonic influence
>   Knowledge of supernatural
>   Supernatural strength
> Features Associated with Both Mental Disorders and Sin
>   Going about naked
>   Fierce, violent behavior
> Unique Features
>   ???
>
> **Table 3**

because a person does not show obvious symptoms such as those listed in Table 2, that he or she is free from demonic influence. Our knowledge of Satan's craftiness should lead us to suspect that just the opposite may be true: demonic influence may be greatest in individuals who seem least likely to be so afflicted. Satan can appear as an angel of light, and he has always had his false teachers and false prophets.[9]

One further issue requires consideration. While we have, so far, thought of demonic influence as falling along a continuum in terms of degree, the biblical accounts of demon possession and the casting out of demons raise the possibility of an important qualitative distinction. These accounts suggest that demons may actually inhabit a person. Does such inhabitation result in a qualitative difference in the nature or degree of influence? Might there be substantial differences between the degree and form of influence when a demon inhabits the person rather than influencing him or her from outside the person's body? Both biblical data and case reports support such a distinction. A critical factor is whether the individual is a Christian; since the unbeliever belongs to Satan it should not be surprising that Satan's emissaries can inhabit or possess the unbeliever. This is not so with the Christian.

The inhabitation of a person by one or more demons results in different forms and degrees of control; this can have significant implications for the treatment process. We will return to this in a later chapter. For now, we will consider how a person comes under demonic influence.

AVENUES INTO DEMONIC INFLUENCE

There are a number of avenues into demonic influence or possession. Central among these are habitual patterns of personal sinfulness and a variety of forms of cultic and occult worship. Though some might dispute it, others include the use of alcohol and street drugs as well as the abuse of legitimate medications among avenues into demonic influence.

Possession of charms and amulets, and of objects associated with occult practices, may also make one open to demonic influence. Horoscopes, tarot cards, Ouija boards, and possibly the game Dungeons and Dragons may be additional avenues into demonic influence. Participation in the contemporary hard rock music culture, especially with such groups as AC/DC and KISS (Knights in Service to Satan) can also be an avenue into demonic influence.

A central theme in practices which lead persons into demonic influence is an unwillingness to accept God's sovereign control over the conditions of life, including health, possessions, relationships to others, status and social influence, and knowledge of the future. As was discussed earlier, turning to those things rather than to God is false worship, and all false worship involves allegiance to Satan, whether or not we are aware of it.

Doubtless some will question whether one or more of those activities is harmful. Indeed, in some instances individuals likely have participated in some or all of these activities without apparent harm. It is one of the hallmarks of Satan's character that he is able to corrupt and pervert even such things as music, art, or medication, which, used rightly, are holy and right and good.

Sexuality is one example of this perversion of God's good creation by Satan. God created us as sexual beings. The sexual relationship within marriage was pronounced as holy and pure; it is a mutual obligation of marital partners to each other (1 Cor. 7:1–5). Most commentators believe that a central theme of the book of Song of Solomon is celebration of sexual intimacy in marriage.

Yet, we find accounts in Scripture and in society around us countless forms of perverted sexual behavior: fornication, adultery, homosexual practices, bestiality (zoophilia), rape, and sexual abuse. Even the withholding of what is due the marriage partner is a perversion of sexuality, sometimes carried out in the mistaken belief that Scripture teaches that sex is for procreation alone.

In addition to the possibility of persons choosing to commit sexual sin, there is also the possibility of demonic influence or possession playing a role in sexual activities. This seems particularly likely when the activities are of such a compulsive nature that the person seems unable to control them, or when they take some of the more extreme forms, such as sexual sadism, sexual abuse of children, and child pornography.

Personal sin is a key element in most cases of demonization. However, some believe that demons may come to control a person apart from any personal volition or action, coming instead through the occult sins of the parents.

Dickason refers to this as "ancestral influence." He argues that bondage, mediumistic abilities, and demonization are not passed genetically. "However, if the parents back to the third or fourth generation were involved in the occult or had demonic abilities, then the children may be affected or even invaded as a legal judgment from God."[10]

Dickason reports that as many as 95 percent of cases of demonic influence, in his experience, are the result of involvement with demons by ancestors. He believes that the boy who was demonized from childhood is such a case.[11]

That demonic influence occurs in several generations in the same family seems quite likely. However, Dickason's view of ancestral influence seems doubtful. He bases his conclusion on an interpretation of Exodus 20:3–6, which refers to God's "visiting the iniquity of the fathers on the children, on the third and fourth generations of those who hate Me, but showing lovingkindness to thousands [of generations], to those who love Me and keep My commandments." Dickason misinterprets this passage. Its focus is on God's mercy to those who obey him, mercy to "thousands of generations" of descendants of those who keep God's ways. God's dealing with the descendants of King David illustrates God's faithfulness in carrying out this promise. Further, other scriptural passages make it clear that sinful patterns are passed through families by the normal processes of learning and social influence rather than by inheritance (or "ancestral influence").

Finally, there is nothing in the Gospel text to support Dickason's claim that the boy who was demonized from childhood became that way through ancestral influence; if anything, the text points away from this conclusion since his father brought him to Jesus for deliverance; further, in response to Jesus he said: "I do believe; help my unbelief."

It is important to be aware that Satan and demons are not passive agents. They are actively involved in seeking to gain influence over people, and they employ a variety of strategies toward this end. Among Satan's ploys are temptation, accusation, deception, harassment, bodily harm of all persons, and possession of unbelievers.[12]

We will return to the question of avenues into the demonic again in chapter 9 when we examine behavioral indicators of possible demonic influence. In summary, all false worship provides a possible means of coming under control of demonic influence since it involves, as we saw in chapter 4, knowing or unwitting worship of Satan. Similarly, all other forms of sinful activity, especially when repeated or habitual, provide an avenue for coming under demonic influence since they involve giving that object or activity the respect, status, and importance that rightfully belongs to God alone (Exod. 20:1–6). In effect, these too are forms of false worship and lead one directly to Satan and the demonic.

Dickason notes that "moral responsibility for continuing in the state of possession and for acts committed while in that state stands as a clouded issue."[13] The problem is that the individual is not in control when the demon(s) exercise control, and in some instances the individual may be so effectively disabled mentally by the demon(s) that he or she is unable to seek help, perhaps even unable to recognize his or her plight.

It is noteworthy that in some ways this conclusion regarding the responsibility of the demon possessed parallels the reasoning behind contemporary laws providing that persons may be found "not guilty by reason of insanity" or "guilty and insane."

In either case, the treatment of choice has been psychiatric/psychological treatment rather than imprisonment. The view that the possessed person has diminished mental and volitional capacities also parallels beliefs that once persons have begun to drink, those who are genetically predisposed to alcoholism may be unable to stop, and may have greatly lessened abilities to think rationally or to act morally as well.

It is important to remember that demon possession occurs only in the unsaved. However, while the demon-possessed person has had his or her mind blinded, we must remember that this person has reached this state through a variety of conscious decisions involving choosing to come under demonic influence. The Christian, with the indwelling Holy Spirit, belongs to God's kingdom, thus is protected from possession, and has the resources through the body of Christ and the power of the Holy Spirit to resist Satan's efforts (compare Ephesians 2:1–6; Colossians 1:13–14 with Ephesians 6:12–18).

LIMITATIONS OF POSSESSION ACCOUNTS IN SCRIPTURE

Biblical accounts of demon possession are limited. We cannot assume that Jesus delivered all those afflicted with demon possession in his day. It seems likely that Jesus delivered only those who were brought to seek his aid, or who came into contact with him for other reasons. There must have been many in Israel during the life of Jesus who were demonically influenced or possessed, but who did not receive deliverance.

For several reasons our concept of demonic influence should not be limited to what may be gleaned from the biblical accounts of demon possession, though it must be guided by them.

First, these stories may intentionally address only selected issues. An analogy to biblical teachings regarding the church may be helpful here. Basic principles about the nature and purpose of the church are revealed, and examples of how it functioned are presented. However, much is left unsaid; this encourages the search for Spirit-led wisdom in adapting the church to different times and cultures.

Similarly, in the case of the demonic, basic principles regarding the demonic are given in Scripture, providing an important interpretive framework for understanding the specifics of contemporary cases of demonic influence or possession. The alternative is to develop our demonology from the reports of demons themselves; this is most dangerous since they are by their very nature liars and deceivers.

Second, it appears that the primary purpose of the Gospel accounts of deliverance from demonic influence was to demonstrate the coming of the kingdom of God and the person of Jesus Christ. The focus, then, is on the person and character of Christ rather than on the nature and manifestations of demons. Put more strongly, the foremost purpose of Scripture is to teach us about God, though teaching about demons may also be included.

Third, as noted in chapter 3, there are numerous accounts of satanic and demonic influence reported in the Gospels in places other than in stories of demon possession. This underscores the importance of distinguishing these conditions.

Fourth, as noted above, it seems extremely doubtful that Jesus expelled demons from all who were afflicted in Palestine in his day, any more than it is plausible to believe that he healed all who were sick of various diseases. It seems likely that these miracles were performed as signs of the presence of the kingdom of God on earth. This raises doubt about whether miraculous healings and castings out are part of God's usual mode of action. Further, Christ gives no indication that it was his purpose to seek out and deliver all who were possessed by Satan or demons.

Fifth, we must ponder what differences existed between those who were delivered from demons by Jesus and those who were not delivered. Many factors may distinguish such individuals. Jesus apparently delivered only those who were brought to him for help at their own initiative or the initiative of others, and those who came in contact with him because of curiosity or possibly other reasons. This may be an important factor to keep in mind as we seek to deal with similar phenomena today.

Sixth, Satan's methods are varied. There are several reasons why demonic influence or demonization may not be typical for Satan's current mode of activity in the United States, though this appears to be rapidly changing. It appears that there have been special outpourings of satanic activity in the form of overt demonization at certain times in human history. These outpourings appear to coincide with significant manifestations of the power of God at work in human history and with the shifts in God's modes of activity in human history. Some believe that the outpouring of demonic manifestations during the life of Christ was unprecedented.[14] This should not be too surprising since the death and resurrection of Christ represented a pivotal victory for God. That Satan should mount an unprecedented campaign at such a time is only to be expected.

Another major factor that may account for the relatively low frequency of possession in recent history in the United States is the fact that Christianity has historically been the dominant religious system in the U.S. Moreover, the recent growth of religious pluralism in the U.S. may, in turn, account for the apparent increase in reports of possession. Thiessen notes that the possessions with which Jesus dealt involved persons from outlying districts, persons who were half gentile; such phenomena apparently were not seen in the environs of Jerusalem, where reverence of God was more common.[15]

A final factor that might account for differences between the biblical accounts and current manifestations of satanic influence is that Satan may well vary his tactics with time and culture. As a deceiver who can appear even as an angel of light, it should be no surprise that Satan would choose tactics which are least likely to attract attention to his activities.

Much in Scripture suggests that even in the time of Christ Satan manifested himself in other more subtle ways, as well as in overt influence or possession.

DEMON POSSESSION IN OTHER CULTURES

Getting an accurate picture of the occurrences of demonic influence in other cultures is difficult. Most accounts of demonic influence from such settings are in the form of case histories and anecdotal stories, many of which may be distorted by memory failure and inaccurate perceptions. However, some tentative conclusions may be drawn. In many instances, those who profess to be involved in the demonic in Third World settings do not seem to show the same characteristics discovered in biblical accounts of possession. Often these individuals also lack the features that would likely result in their being diagnosed with a mental disorder.

For instance, witch doctors, shamans, fakirs, and magicians have great power and influence in their cultures. They are feared, revered, and respected. Rather than manifesting loss of reality contact, they appear to be knowledgeable, clever, resourceful, crafty, and cunning. Those whom Jesus delivered from demonic influence were quite different from these persons. The ones Christ delivered were generally outcasts, unable to function effectively in society. In contrast, the behavior of Simon, the magician of Samaria (Acts 8:18–25), and the fortune teller of Philippi (Acts 16:11–22), appear to be more similar to the contemporary patterns of demonic influence as seen in Third World cultures.

What conclusions may be drawn from these observations?

First, we should be aware that much of what the Bible has to say about demonic influence has often been overlooked by those who focus narrowly on demon possession. Such a narrow focus reveals only a limited picture of Satan and his influence. Remember that Jesus characterized the Pharisees as belonging to Satan. Also, Paul was afflicted by a messenger from Satan.

Second, we must recognize that to distinguish between mental disorders and demonic influence we must seek to understand all the symptoms and forms of demonic influence.

SUMMARY

In seeking to understand the characteristics of demon possession, most writers have focused on accounts of casting out demons during the ministry of Jesus as recorded in the New Testament Gospels. However, the signs of demonic influence in these accounts are similar to those associated with mental disorders.

In approaching the question of whether the Gospel accounts of possession give an adequate basis for discovering the forms of demonic influence, several limitations of these accounts have been identified: 1) they provide an interpretive framework rather than providing exhaustive information about the influences of demons; 2) their emphasis is on showing the presence and power of Christ; 3) there is much evidence throughout Scripture that demons also operate in other ways; 4) it is doubtful that Jesus cast out demons from all those so afflicted in Palestine in his day; 5) Jesus only cast demons out of those who were brought for his help or with whom he came into contact for reasons such as curiosity; 6) Satan's methods vary with time and culture.

Accounts of demonism in Third World cultures, and of demonic influence in other biblical passages, suggest a great variety of characteristics of people under demonic influence. Often the demon possessed are individuals of power and influence who are respected, revered, and even feared. Thus, we should be cautious about concluding that all instances of demonic influence will exhibit the symptoms most often associated with demon possession in the Gospels. Unfortunately, that fact complicates the issue of the relationship between demonic influence and mental disorders.

If these conclusions about the effects of demonic influence are accurate, then the tendency to view demonic influence and mental disorders as alternate explanations for the same phenomena needs to be reconsidered. It is to this issue that we turn in chapter 8.

CHAPTER EIGHT

DEMONIC INFLUENCE AND MENTAL DISORDERS

Earlier we saw that demon possession was a widely accepted explanation for disturbed behavior from antiquity through the middle of the nineteenth century. The scientific revolution and the adoption of naturalistic reductionism around the close of the nineteenth century left no room for the supernatural or spiritual. Consequently, what had formerly been viewed as demonic influence became "nothing but" mental illness or mental disorders.[1]

The belief that demon possession is merely a misunderstanding of mental illness has created considerable discomfort for persons committed to a biblical worldview; the Bible clearly states that demons are real and that they are evidenced in both powerful and dramatic ways, at least under some circumstances. How can a more literal view of Scripture be reconciled with the now-prevailing naturalistic view of mental disorders?

In exploring the relationship between demonic influences and mental disorders, we must remember that the question is not whether Satan is involved in mental disorders; rather, it is a question of how he is involved.

Mental disorders, like any other human malady, came with the Fall and the entrance of sin into the world. All human suffering can be traced, in part, to that momentous event. Satan's role in the Fall, and thus in all earthly ill, must be acknowledged. Discerning the means of his involvement in mental disorders is the issue at hand.

Historically, the predominant view has been that demon possession and mental disorders are alternative explanations of the same phenomena. However, from a Christian perspective they are distinct. Therefore, we need first of all to ask whether, on the basis of their respective symptoms alone, we can tell the difference between demon possession and mental illness. Next we will consider what information may be missed if we evaluate only symptoms. Finally, we will look at two alternative approaches to understanding the relationship between mental disorders and demonic possession.

As we examine the relationship of demonic influence and possession to mental disorders, it is important to keep in mind several considerations. The first consideration must be that of distinguishing among spiritual, psychological, and physical problems.

Second, given our assumption that mental disorders and demon possession both occur, we must realize that a given person may show any of the following conditions: 1) physical disorder alone; 2) demon possession alone; 3) mental disorder alone; 4) a combination of physical disorder, demon possession, and mental disorder. Demon possession is understood to be a spiritual problem, while a mental disorder is a psychological problem.

Third, it is important to remember that Satan was involved in the entrance of sin into our world, and thus in the many changes that resulted. Whether the problem is spiritual, psychological, physical, or a combination of these, Satan is nonetheless involved.

117

COMPARISON OF DEMONIC INFLUENCE AND
MENTAL DISORDERS

As Christians became increasingly interested in psychology during the sixties and seventies, several Christian authors grappled with the question of how to distinguish demon possession from mental disorders. They focused on comparing and contrasting the symptoms of mental disorders with the symptoms of demon possession as described in the Gospel accounts. One of the first things they noticed was the extent to which the symptoms of the two conditions overlap.

Virkler and Virkler suggest that the Scripture reflects a consistent distinction between demonic and disease symptoms, both in language and treatment (casting out versus healing).[2] However, other discussions of the nature and manifestation of demonic influence suggest that distinctions between demonic symptoms and symptoms of mental or physical illnesses are not clearly drawn in Scripture. J. Ramsey Michaels says that in the Gospel of Mark a fairly distinct line is preserved between healing and exorcism, but that Matthew and Luke blur this line and seem to categorize them together, as does Peter in Acts. Michaels concludes that a tendency to extend or extrapolate the definition of the demonic to include other phenomena besides actual possession, or to subsume possession under illness, was already present in the New Testament writings.[3]

Several incidents illustrate this ambiguity. The Jewish rulers accused Jesus of having a demon (see Matt. 12:22–29; Mark 3:20–27; John 7:20; 8:48–52; 10:19–21). Perhaps more significantly, the possibility that Jesus was mentally ill was raised on two of these same occasions, once by his own family (Mark 3:21) and once by the Jews (John 10:19–21). Thus, even in the time of Christ there appears to have been confusion regarding the distinctions between mental illness and demonic influence (and these were both confused with signs of the power of God).

Bloesch proposes a distinction in terms of the mind and the will: he suggests that mental disorders affect the mind, while demonic influence affects the will.[4] However, if we examine the scriptural accounts of possession, such as that of the Gadarene demoniac or the fortune teller, we notice that their minds seem to have been affected (Mark 5:1–20; Acts 16:16–18; 2 Cor. 4:4).

Similarly, examination of mental disorders suggests that in some mental disorders the will may be affected; examples include severe depression and perhaps alcoholism and drug dependence. In other mental disorders the primary disturbance is one of affect or emotion, as in the major affective disorders, and most neurotic disorders. In practice, people function as wholes, with a continuous interplay among mind, will and emotions in a manner that makes it impossible to sustain the functional distinction required by Bloesch's formulation.[5]

In another attempt to distinguish between demon possession and mental disorders, Sall contrasted demons and mental illness, postulating several distinctions between them.[6] In commenting on Sall's view, Bach terms it a curious comparison; Bach suggests comparing the psychotic with the demon-possessed person rather than with the demon.[7] I heartily concur.

In practical terms we must observe the person who shows disturbed behavior and determine whether or not a demon is present. Demons do not readily reveal their presence for analysis and treatment; if we knew beforehand that the person had a demon, then there would be no difficulty in distinguishing demonic influence from mental disorders.

Comparison of the two conditions reveals that virtually all of the symptoms associated with demonic influence are duplicated in at least one mental disorder as defined by DSM-III-R.

Supernatural knowledge is often claimed by individuals with the hallucinations and delusions of psychotic disorders, especially paranoid schizophrenics. Exploits of unusual strength and endurance may be observed in manic episodes and in catatonic conditions (where normal fatigue reactions seem to be absent). Nakedness or deterioration of dress and appearance is common in the psychotic disorders, especially in schizophrenia.

Loss of speech and hearing, and blindness, along with a number of other physical symptoms, are characteristic of the Conversion (hysterical) Disorders. Seizures occur in epilepsy and a variety of other disorders: "Most of the etiological agents underlying chronic brain syndromes can and do cause convulsions, particularly syphilis, intoxication, trauma, cerebral arteriosclerosis, and intracranial neoplasms."[8]

Speaking in a different voice, and even the appearance of two or more distinct personalities are classified as Dissociative Disorders (e.g., Multiple Personality Disorder). Bizarre behavior is characteristic of all of the psychotic conditions. Finally, fierce and violent behavior is found in certain psychotic conditions, especially Delusional (paranoid) Disorder, as well as in Intermittent Explosive Disorder, Antisocial Personality, and Conduct Disorders of Childhood and Adolescence.

Those who are demon possessed sometimes admit that fact. Claims to be demon possessed are specifically included as a consideration in the diagnosis of Multiple Personality Disorder.[9]

Finally, persons who are demon possessed often show involvement in occult practices; while this activity is not a defining symptom for any specific mental disorder, it seems likely that it could be observed in persons diagnosed with a number of disorders.

Demonic influence and mental disorders are conceptually distinct phenomena, but in view of the extensive overlap among symptoms, it may be difficult in a given instance to make a firm conclusion regarding which phenomenon is present. Table 4 summarizes the comparison between these two patterns of symptoms.

One final observation is that there is also similarity between organic and nonorganic mental disorders. For example, disorientation, mental confusion, and depressed mood may be the result of such organic causes as exposure to toxic chemicals or a minor stroke, or may result from nonorganic factors, such as a psychotic depressive condition. Thus, it is important to remember that similarity in symptoms does not necessarily mean that the sources of the symptoms are identical. Nor does it necessarily mean that the symptoms are identical in all respects.

In summary, Table 4 indicates that virtually all of the symptoms of demon possession found in the Gospel accounts can conceivably be classified within one of the mental disorders. From this we might conclude that mental disorders and demonic influence are conceptually distinct, but that one cannot tell the difference between them in most instances, and that it does not

Comparison of Demonic Influence and Mental Disorders[15]	
Characteristics of Demonic Influence	**Parallels among Mental Disorders**
Supernatural knowledge	Hallucinations, delusions of psychotic disorders; God told me . . ., etc. (Also note parallels with psychics)
Supernatural strength	Observed in manic episodes, certain psychotic conditions; e.g. catatonic does not show normal fatigue.
Going about naked	Deterioration of appearance and social graces is typical of psychotic disorders, especially schizophrenia, and of schizotypal personality disorder
Unable to hear, speak; blind	Associated with conversion (hysterical) disorders
Seizures	Observed with epilepsy and many chronic brain syndromes such as syphilis, intoxication, trauma, cerebral arteriosclerosis, and intracranial neoplasms
Use of "different" voice; presence of distinct personality	Commonly found in dissociative disorders, which include multiple personality disorder
Bizarre behavior	Characteristic of psychoses
Fierce, violent behavior	Common in certain psychotic conditions, especially, paranoid; also found in intermittent explosive disorder, antisocial personality, and unsocialized aggressive reaction of childhood or adolescence
Claims of demonic influence	Found in multiple personality disorder
Involvement in occult practices	May occur with many disorders, though not used as diagnostic criterion

Table 4

make a great deal of difference in treatment. However, this view is too simplistic, as we shall see.

It seems clear that this striking similarity between mental disorders and demon possession as portrayed in the Gospels is a primary factor accounting for both versions of the current view that they are different explanations for the same phenomenon. The first version holds that demon possession is an archaic explanation of mental disorders. This view involves materialistic reductionism, a philosophy that is prevalent among non-Christians in the Western world. Curiously, it is also held by many who profess to be Christians.

A second approach to the obvious similarity of demon possession and mental disorders emphasizes demon possession and the need for deliverance. Proponents of this view believe that the only legitimate mental disorders are those which are of clear organic origins, and that such disorders are quite rare. This view tends toward a spiritualistic reductionism and leaves no room for problems such as those of Leila, who had developed some very harmful attitudes and behavior; nor does it leave room for such things as the fear of others which results from being abused as a child by drunken parents. Those who take this approach are often among the more charismatic Christian groups, though many others hold this view as well.

Neither of these first views is satisfactory since each involves a form of reductionism that is far too simplistic. A third view is that mental disorders and demon possession are distinct phenomena, though they are similar in their symptoms. This view seems to better fit the evidence which we have reviewed so far. If correct, it implies that a person may be: 1) demon possessed, 2) mentally disordered, or 3) both demon possessed and mentally disordered, at the same time or at different times.

FACTORS OTHER THAN SYMPTOMS

The reasoning that mental disorders and demonic influence are almost indistinguishable seems to make sense, particularly when we examine the symptoms reported in the Gospel accounts. However, merely examining symptoms ignores differences in causes. When we fail to distinguish the conditions, we will not treat them in the distinct manners which their different origins may warrant. For example, a person may be mentally confused and delirious due to demon possession, a brain tumor, epilepsy, or a variety of other factors. Precise diagnosis is critical to appropriate treatment. Thus, it is important to discover ways in which the two conditions can be distinguished.

Several factors suggest that the two conditions are distinct. First, spiritual and psychological functioning are distinct, though inseparable. Second, demonic influence in other cultures sometimes occurs without the symptoms associated with mental disorders. Third, Satan is a deceiver who uses a variety of methods to accomplish his ends. Fourth, biological factors are often involved in mental disorders. Fifth, deliberate personal evil is sometimes involved in a person's coming under satanic influence. Finally, personal faith is an important factor limiting demonic influence. We shall examine each of these in turn.

Spiritual and Psychological Are Distinct

Demonic influence or possession is primarily a spiritual condition, while mental disorders are primarily psychological. As we have just seen, two major views conclude that these conditions are indistinguishable; both involve reductionism. They suggest that people have spiritual problems, or that they have psychological problems, but never both. We need to remember that men and women are multidimensional beings. Thus, it seems likely that problems can occur in any dimension—spiritual, psychological, or physical. Often a given problem may involve more than a single dimension.

Demon Possession in Other Cultures

As noted earlier, those who profess or exhibit demon possession in other cultures often do not seem to show signs of impaired functioning or loss of reality orientation which characterize severe mental disorders (the clinical syndromes). They seem well-oriented to their culture and quite capable of functioning in society. On the other hand, there may be some similarity between these individuals and those classified with personality disorders in DSM-III-R, as we shall see later.[11]

We must be cautious here since many believe that personality disorders form the basic personality structure and functioning that underlie particular types of mental disorders. Examination of the personality disorders suggests that, except in mild form, even they seem to involve qualities inconsistent with the more common manifestations associated with demonic influence in other cultures.[12]

Satan's Character

Another reason for highlighting distinctions between mental disorders and demonic influence involves the nature and character of Satan. Satan is a deceiver who seeks to hide his working in a variety of ways. Thus, it is not surprising that demonic influence or possession sometimes appears much like mental or physical disorders, and that such similarity may be most common in Western culture where there is a high degree of concern with mental and physical disorders.

However, in many Third World cultures where there is a tendency to attribute just about every problem to demonic influence, even the most obviously physical ailments, such as dysentery, may be helplessly accepted because they are believed to be of demonic or spiritual origin. This contrasts with our Western tendency to explain all human problems in physical and psychological terms. Both of these tendencies result in misdiagnosis and ineffective treatment. Much human suffering results.

Biological Factors in Mental Disorder

The growing evidence of the role of biological factors in many mental disorders casts further doubt on the view that mental disorders and demonic influence are the same phenomenon.

A person whose function is impaired by an organic disorder is not likely to be optimally effective as an agent for Satan's purposes. Because of impaired thinking or perception, and other functional abilities, persons with schizophrenic or other psychotic disorders often lose the ability to care for themselves even in rudimentary ways. While Satan can, and no doubt often does, use such individuals to accomplish his purposes, those with more intact psychological functioning are apt to be more effective agents of his nefarious goals. While not a strong argument, this lends further support to the view that Satan may accomplish his ends more effectively through other means than causing people to become mentally disordered.

Further, Developmental Disorders, Gender Identity Disorders, Psychoactive Substance-Use Disorders, and Mood Disorders are all believed to be at least partially the result of biological predisposing factors such as genetic anomalies and biochemical disturbances. This type of disorder is produced by an interaction between the biological predisposition and psychosocial experiences.

In general, it seems safe to presume that demonic influence is relatively independent of biological causes, such as those just described. If this is true, it follows that as evidence of organic cause increases, the likelihood of demonic influence as an explanation for behavioral disturbance is correspondingly decreased. It is noteworthy that those mental disorders that are characterized by the most prominent disturbances of thought and behavior are also the conditions to which biological factors have been most strongly linked. This suggests that psychotic manifestations—mental disorders in which disturbed religious ideation is quite common—are unlikely to be the result of demonic influence because of the high probability of organic causes such as senile dementia. Thus, the deranged person who claims to be Jesus Christ, Napoleon, or Satan is more likely to have a severe organic brain disorder or schizophrenic disorder than a demon.

Two important cautionary notes must be sounded here. First, because all aspects of the person interact, it is possible that malfunction in one of them may result in greater vulnerability to stressors that could interfere with functioning in other dimensions. Just as physical illness makes a person more prone to depression, so depression may make a person more likely to become demonically influenced. The fact that one problem leads to another does not negate the value of distinguishing among the conditions, both for conceptualization and treatment.

Second, we have seen that Satan is able to produce even physical disorders, as well as physical healings. Thus, while the presence of physical factors often makes the probability of demon possession seem less likely, it cannot clearly rule out the demonic factor.

Personal Evil

Personal evil is a complex issue. It is clear from DSM-III-R that volition is involved to some degree in many mental disorders. Factitious Disorders, for example, are defined as "physical or psychological symptoms that are intentionally produced or feigned."[13] A voluntary component may also be involved in Somatoform Disorders[14] and Dissociative Disorders. In fact, it is believed that the symptoms of most mental disorders may be

125

voluntarily exaggerated for personal benefit; often this is referred to as "secondary gain."

Another category of mental disorder that involves personal volition is drug and alcohol abuse or dependence. For some individuals such dependence grows out of medical treatment for pain, injury, or illness. For most, it begins with the choice to drink, smoke, snort, or inject the substance. It is now widely believed that, regardless of how the habit first began, biological factors play an important role in determining which individuals will become dependent upon drugs or alcohol. However, for most, volition plays at least a minor role; had they never participated to begin with, abuse or dependence never would have developed.

There is considerable controversy regarding the relationship between personal volition and mental disorders. The relationship between volition and demonic influence is similarly complex. King Saul, for example, chose to disobey God, and as a consequence God's spirit departed from him (see 1 Samuel 16:14). But was not Saul's affliction by the evil spirit an unanticipated consequence of his sin, much as becoming an alcoholic is an unanticipated result of choosing to drink alcoholic beverages?

It seems likely that in most cases the person has made a clear, conscious choice that leads to influence or control by demons. Often the person does not initially recognize the demonic influence; recognition comes later, when the control is well established.

Personal Faith

The role of personal faith is another factor in seeking to discern whether demonic influence is involved. A number of Scriptures warn of the need to be on guard and to arm ourselves for protection from the evil one. These make it clear that a Christian can be influenced by Satan (Eph. 6:12–17; 1 Pet. 5:8– 9). It also seems clear that faith in God and faithful obedience to God are important factors in protection from the power of Satan and his emissaries (Rev. 12:11). It is important at this point to remember that all false worship is ultimately worship of demons, and of their chief, Satan.

Some have argued that it is not possible for a Christian to be demon possessed, although a believer could be harassed or influenced by a demon. Others, such as Unger and Dickason, suggest that there is good reason to believe that Christians can be demon possessed; they profess to have delivered countless Christians from this very problem.[15]

Dickason argues first that the Bible does not rule out demonic influence of Christians today. He objects to "the assumption that demons do not operate in demonization as much today, that they change their tactics, or that their influence has faded away. Nothing in the New Testament supports such an assumption."[16] He then concludes that the Bible leaves open the possibility of demonic possession of believers, and that clinical data confirms that Christians may be, and sometimes are, demonically possessed.

Many disagree with Dickason regarding possession of believers.[17] His evidence, which is largely from case histories, is not compelling.

I believe that possession of Christians is not possible since they belong to the kingdom of God, and are indwelt by the Holy Spirit. Also, God protects them from the evil one. However, I believe the evidence is unequivocal that even as Christ himself was accosted and harassed during his earthly life, so believers today may be also; they may even be attacked by demons. Thus, it is imperative that we take seriously the matter of spiritual warfare regardless of our position on the matter of demonic possession of believers.

Other Problems

Accepting the conclusion that mental disorders and demonic influence are indistinguishable presents other problems. Chief among these is that if we are unable to distinguish them, then different approaches to treatment are precluded. Yet it seems clear that mental disorders and demonic influence, having different origins, need different treatment approaches. The medical concept of diagnosis is based on the belief that different problems, such as delirium tremens, epileptic seizures, and rapidly growing brain tumors, require different treatment. That reasoning seems to apply here as well: Psychological problems and spiritual problems presumably belong to different categories, though they interact. If this is correct, then it follows that treatment may be different as well.

ALTERNATIVE VIEWS

Allison's and Schwarz's View

Allison is a psychiatrist who has specialized in treating Multiple Personality Disorders. He and Schwarz distinguish five levels or grades of possession. Their view is consistent with the notion that demonic influence varies along a continuum from minimal influence to full possession. According to them, Grade I possession involves control "by an idea, obsession, involuntary act, compulsion or addiction to alcohol or drugs."[18] "It could also be labelled obsessive-compulsive neurosis. . . ."[19]

Grade II possession occurs in persons with multiple personality: "[It] is the result of the influence of a negative alter personality developed by a person with hysterical personality structure."[20] This sort corresponds to the proverbial Dr. Jekyll and Mr. Hyde.

> In many cultures the alter personality would be considered a classic example of an evil spirit invading the body of (the person). (However), with adequate information from (the) unconscious, there is no need to invoke supernatural explanations.[21]

In Grade III possessions "the controlling influence seems to be the mind of another living human being."[22]

Grade IV possession is control by the spirit of another human being.

"Grade V possession is control by a spirit that has never had its own life history and identifies itself as an agent of evil. . . . Only the power of God and his angels can conquer such entities."[23]

Allison and Schwarz seem to believe that Multiple Personality Disorder, at least, develops chiefly as a method of coping with abusive experiences during early childhood. This suggests that these persons whom they consider to be least severely possessed are the victims of the sinfulness of others.

After describing the relationship between mental disorders and demonism, Allison concludes, "I can only reiterate my own belief. . . . Are patients really possessed? I don't know."[24] Despite this cautious conclusion, and Allison's and Schwarz's care in making assertions at times, it seems clear they believe that the spirit world is real. Allison's and Schwarz's view seems somewhat unorthodox. Yet they are among a very few who openly acknowledge phenomena which do not easily fit the mental disorder model.

Personality Disorders

Another possible relationship between mental disorders and demon possession is the suggestion that demon possession may occur in those with personality disorders. Personality traits are enduring patterns of perceiving, relating to, and thinking about oneself, others, and the world about us. Only when these patterns become inflexible and maladaptive are they termed personality disorders. Often these patterns develop in childhood, lasting into the adult years. The key element in personality disorders which suggests a link with the demonic is the pervasive sense of self-centeredness and unconcern for others which is inherent in the more extreme forms of these disorders.

Antisocial Personality Disorder Antisocial Personality Disorder is characterized by a wide variety of irresponsible and antisocial acts, such as lying, stealing, vandalism, sexual promiscuity, instigating fights, and physical cruelty. Most of these patterns of behavior are likely to lead to arrest and prosecution on criminal charges.

Those with these patterns typically feel no remorse, and often feel justified in their actions. Further, they are unlikely to seek help voluntarily, thus are rarely seen in mental-health treatment settings except when sent there by the courts or other powerful persons involved in their lives, such as spouses or bosses. Many of the patterns which might lead to a person's being diagnosed with an Antisocial Personality Disorder are also common among persons with demonic influence, as we shall see later. In the personality disorders, then, we may have a point of contact between mental disorders and demonic influence.

Narcissistic Personality Disorder The Narcissistic Personality Disorder is characterized by extreme need for self-importance, insensitivity to the needs, wants, or feelings of others, extreme sensitivity to the least slight or offense from others, and strong desire to be "special," often alternating with periods of feeling unworthy. While not showing the blatantly antisocial characteristics of the antisocial personality, the narcissistic personality is, nonetheless, extremely self-centered and more subtly devalues, exploits, or harms others; the focus for the narcissist is on psychic rather than material benefits. Persons with narcissistic personalities seem to fit the pattern of those whom Peck terms "truly evil people." Here, too, there is a possible avenue into the demonic, though it is more subtle, involving primarily acts of omission rather than of commission.

Schizotypal Personality Disorder Those with Schizotypal Personality Disorder (formerly simple schizophrenia) are odd in appearance, thought, and behavior, and show little interest or skill in social relationships. Among other features, persons with this disorder often show "magical thinking"; they may believe that they can read the thoughts and feelings of others or that others can read their minds. They also report sensing the presence of persons or forces unseen by others.[25]

In addition to possible links with Antisocial, Narcissistic, and Schizotypal Personality Disorders, Allison and Schwarz have suggested that possession may be associated with Obsessive-Compulsive Disorder, and Multiple Personality Disorders at their levels I and II; they propose no mental disorders which correspond to more advanced possession.

Thus, in addition to Obsessive-Compulsive and Multiple Personality Disorder (a Dissociative Disorder coded on the first dimension in DSM-III), personality disorders (coded on dimension 2) are another point at which mental disorders and demonic influence may overlap. Personality disorders lack clear biological causes, and exhibit the presence of volitional evil either in the form of evil actions by the person, or in the form of being victimized by the evil of another.

SUMMARY

From antiquity, disturbances of behavior and conduct have been explained in religious terms. With the rise of naturalism in the late nineteenth century a dramatic shift occurred, and the same phenomena came to be labeled mental disorders and explained in terms of natural causes. Demonic influence and mental disorders have continued to be viewed as alternative explanations for the same symptomatic manifestations.

An analysis of the demon-possession accounts suggests that most of those symptomatic manifestations are also considered to be symptomatic of one or more mental disorders. As a consequence of this overlap in manifestations, many conclude that we merely have two labels and explanations for the same phenomena. Some of those who believe that there is but one phenomenon with two labels deny the demonic and affirm only naturalistic explanations; this view is common among both non-Christian and Christian groups. Others, especially charismatic Christians, affirm demonic influence and discount naturalistic causes.

A third view is that mental disorders and demon possession are both real, but not readily distinguishable from each other on the basis of symptoms. This view is consistent with the results of efforts to compare mental disorders with demon-possession accounts in Scripture, but such a proposition is unsatisfactory. It confuses the sources of psychological and spiritual problems, and thus makes it very difficult to provide the different treatments required by their different causes.

Evidence from those Biblical accounts of demonic influence which are separate from the accounts of casting out of demons, and evidence from reports of demonic influence or possession in other cultures, suggest that the forms of demonic influence may be more varied than is apparent from the possession accounts alone. Further, evidence is growing that biological factors play a significant role in mental disorders, while those factors are presumed to be of limited importance in demonic influence.

Finally, personal evil and personal faith clearly play a dominant role in demonic influence. By contrast, they presumably play a limited role in most mental disorders, especially those with significant organic components. However, in Antisocial, Narcissistic, and Schizotypal Personality Disorders, and possibly in some other Personality Disorders (Axis II), there seems to be a significant volitional aspect, and there may be a corresponding overlap between these disorders and demonic influence.

Demon possession and mental disorders are distinct phenomena, though they may occur together and interact with one another. They also have many similarities, particularly in the more extreme forms of demonic influence commonly termed demon possession. How then can they be distinguished? It is to this matter that we turn in chapter 9.

CHAPTER NINE

ASSESSMENT AND DIAGNOSIS OF DEMONIC INFLUENCE

Scott Peck, in his discussion of demonic influence, suggests that we should not seek an exclusive diagnosis of either mental disorder or demonic possession. Rather, he proposes that we ask: Is this person mentally ill? Is he or she demonically controlled? Marguerite Shuster agrees. Implicit in their views is the suggestion that there are instances in which the answer is yes to both inquiries.[1]

Fred Dickason also suggests that mental disorders and demonic influence may occur together. He goes on to say that mental disorders and demonic influence are not the same problem in different terms, nor are they different symptoms of a common problem. Demonic influence and mental disorders may co-occur; yet they are different issues requiring different solutions.

However, the two are often confused due to our tendency to use limited categories. In discussing case studies from his own experience, Dickason comments: "Many had a combination of psychological and demonic problems. This may be common, since demons work with men's minds and bodies."[2]

Samuel Southard also believes that mental disorder and demon possession may occur together. In addressing the relationship between mental disorders and demonic influence, Southard began with three key assumptions: 1) demonizing might occur independently of mental illness or neuroses, 2) mental illness or neuroses might occur independently of demonizing, and 3) in some cases there would be a combination of spiritual and psychological disorders.[3]

The views of Peck, Dickason, and Southard are consistent with the view which has been developed in previous chapters. They agree that mental disorders and demonic influence are two distinct phenomena rather than competing explanations for the same phenomena; the two conditions may be significantly different in some instances, but often are similar in their symptoms; each may occur alone, but they also may occur together; finally, each may affect the other.

While demonic influence and mental disorders are distinct, the fact that persons function as psychophysical and spiritual wholes means that problems in any domain may result in, be produced by, or interact with problems in other domains. This is implicitly acknowledged by the common practice of paying pastoral visits to those who are hospitalized due to illness or injury. Though the immediate cause of hospitalization is usually physical, we recognize that people who experience physical difficulties may experience spiritual or psychological difficulties also. Often, the spiritual and psychological difficulties are a result of the physical, but they also may cause the physical problems.

In the same way, while mental disorders and demonic influence are distinct, their symptoms occur together in many instances. Because of similarities in the two conditions, it is often difficult to distinguish them. Clarifying the distinction between the two is the focus of this chapter.

DIFFERENTIAL DIAGNOSIS

James James was known as a mild-mannered man. In his neighborhood he always had a cheerful greeting and helped anyone who asked. His employer reported that there had never been any problems with James at work, and that he was "a model employee." James first came to my attention when he was brought into the hospital by the police. The police had been summoned to James's home by a neighbor after one of James's children slipped out the back door and went crying for help.

As I explored what had led to James's hospitalization, I learned that he had become increasingly despondent during the previous few weeks. Approximately two years earlier he had invested most of his retirement funds in an oil well on the advice of a friend. His mood began to deteriorate following the recent discovery that the well was worthless and all of his retirement funds were lost. James had become increasingly withdrawn and irritable, though only his wife and children seemed to have observed this change.

On the day he was brought to the hospital, James had come home late. It was obvious he had been drinking, something that was out of character. When he came in, his wife and children were watching a program on television. James suddenly began an angry tirade about how evil it was to watch such programs. He became abusive toward the children. When his wife tried to intervene, he threw her across the room and ordered her to keep out of the way, meanwhile calling her a variety of vulgar names. With an axe James proceeded to smash the television into tiny pieces, threatening to use the axe on his wife and children if they interfered. It was into this scene that the police came.

After several days in the hospital it gradually was revealed that James had become increasingly bitter toward the former friend who had recommended the oil-well investment. Recently this bitterness had been made worse because of financial pressures brought on by a strike at work and the consequent reduction in James's income. What brought it all to a head for James was receiving word that he had been referred to a collection agency for default on his credit-card payments. He also feared repossession of his car, on which he owed more than it was worth.

As James's bitterness was further explored, he reported that he had begun work as a twelve-year-old to provide for himself, his mother, and his two sisters. His father, an alcoholic, spent all the family funds on drink and even took James's earnings whenever he had the opportunity. James had vowed that he was never going to let anyone take his money again, and had never forgiven his father, who had died several years previously. While others rarely perceived it because James was a very private person, James was obsessed with achieving financial success and security. He had been proud of his accomplishments until the oil-well fiasco. Now he felt like a failure.

James's pastor had come to see him in the hospital. The pastor was convinced that this man's problem was spiritual. When he learned about the preoccupation with financial matters and longstanding bitterness he wondered if James could be demon possessed. He suggested that maybe James had a demon of bitterness, and that he needed deliverance.

Was this man demon possessed? Was he mentally disordered? Might he be both demon possessed and mentally disordered? Or could it be that his problems were merely habitual sinfulness? This chapter will suggest ways in which these questions can be resolved.

In a rare attempt to examine the differences between those with mental disorders and demon possession, Southard asked members of his class at Fuller Seminary to collect case reports on persons experiencing personal difficulties. The goal was to seek to clarify the distinctions between mental disorder and demonic influence.

Based on the resulting case histories, Southard suggests several distinguishing features of demonization: unusual feelings of apprehension and/or a sense of evil (sometimes reported as a sense of an alien presence) in the presence of the possessed person; unusual behavior, such as feats of strength and strange looks and voices by the person presumably demonized, or actions undermining personal health and vicious attitudes toward self; psychological improvements during or after exorcism. Most of these, as we saw earlier, also occur with mental disorders, thus are of little use in distinguishing the two conditions.

Southard suggests that failure to find a demon (though it is unclear how he proposes to find demons), or absence of improvement following exorcism, is viewed as evidence of the absence of demonic influence.

He hints that inadequacies of reporting may sharpen the distinctions between mental illness and demonic influence in his cases; persons presenting cases as demonic influence may have overlooked details supportive of a mental-disorder diagnosis, and those presenting cases described as mental illness may have overlooked or failed to report information suggestive of demonic influence.[4] He also notes that his theological students had little training in recognizing psychological disorders; it seems likely that they also had little experience or training in recognizing demon possession.

Southard notes a "tension between rational and intuitive approaches to emotional disturbance and demonizing."[5] There is much evidence that we are more likely to find that for which we are looking than to find evidence that is inconsistent with our preconceptions. This is an important observation, since it implies that mental-health specialists are unlikely to look for or discover demonic influence, while counselors who specialize in deliverance or exorcism are unlikely to seek for or recognize the presence of mental disorders. Perhaps this factor accounts for the fact that little attention has been given to developing methods of differential diagnosis.

The two approaches to distinguishing the mental disorders and demonic influence suggested by Southard include using intuitive methods based on the spiritual gift of "discerning the spirits," and seeking to distinguish on the basis of cultural, family, and personal history. A third approach involves "testing the spirits." The next pages will examine each of these approaches.

Discerning the Spirits

In this approach the helper seeks within himself or herself for the guidance of God's Spirit through a "word of wisdom" or "word of knowledge." In some instances, God's guidance is sought in the context of a diligent search of the Scriptures for behavioral patterns and attitudes that distinguish those who are seeking to honor and serve God from those who are not. The basic theological conviction underlying this approach is that God is a discerner of spirits, and that he is able to reveal his omniscient knowledge to the receptive servant.[6]

One basic problem with exercising spiritual discernment is that we are warned that Satan can disguise himself as an angel of light, and that it may be difficult to distinguish his human followers from citizens of the kingdom of God.

This approach has biblical support, and there is little doubt regarding God's ability to know or communicate knowledge about the presence of an evil spirit. However, we must consider carefully the question of whether God chooses to reveal special knowledge such as this since such detailed knowledge about specific individuals is rarely revealed by God. As a general rule, medical, scientific, and theological knowledge comes as a result of carefully studying what has already been revealed.

Further, there is the danger that what the exorcist interprets as indications of the guidance of God are really the exorcist's own thoughts, feelings or reactions. Worse yet, one might ask whether Satan himself, for some sly reason of his own, might prompt the conviction that the person seeking help is demonically influenced.

Dickason emphasizes the complexity of diagnosis, and warns about the tendency to rely too heavily on the spiritualistic approach. He cautions against the desire for mystical, magical, and miraculous methods. Specifically, he notes ". . . we must caution against the use of what some call 'the gift of discernment.'"[7] It is his belief that the gift of discernment was a sign gift for the apostolic era, which is not operative today.

Dickason goes on to suggest that there are persons who have actually come under the influence of demons through the process of seeking such "discernment." His point is that supernatural knowledge can come from Satan as well as from God. We must always beware of seeking that which God chooses not to grant, and of seeking now what God chooses to grant at another time, even when that involves knowledge that might be useful in making decisions about deliverance.

Discerning of spirits is a legitimate approach, but must be used with considerable caution. Special care must be taken to insure that the "victim" and the helper do not develop unrealistic expectations about the effectiveness of this approach.

Testing the Spirits

Testing the spirits is a process that involves directly addressing the presumed demons, commanding them in the name of Jesus Christ to acknowledge their presence, and to state their name and rank. Dickason proposes that in the name of Jesus we command the evil spirit to come forth and acknowledge its presence, state its name, and give its rank. He believes that since God has won a major victory over Satan in the resurrection, and Satan and demons are thus subject to his control, they must respond to this use of his authority. At the same time, however, Dickason acknowledges in his case illustrations that they do so only grudgingly and with many delays. Thus, even Dickason acknowledges that this approach is not fail-safe.

Talking with demons is not recommended. Runge, for example, warns that "holding a dialogue with [demons] is not only unproductive, it is dangerous."[8] Demons are known liars. Runge argues that demons may enjoy such encounters with would-be exorcists who do not know how to deal effectively with them. He reports:

> I have become convinced that many exorcisms are power play setups by the demons themselves. They choose an exorcist who may lack the wisdom, the knowledge or the authority to challenge them effectively. They choose the timing as well as the audience. The whole process is under their control from the beginning to the end.[9]

Runge describes a personal experience in which manifestations of demonic influence disappeared when a skeptical professional was present, and reappeared after the individual left. He tells of another in which the demons convinced the exorcist to have those present stop praying.

Behavioral Indicators

The behavioral approach combines naturalistic observation of the person and his or her circumstances with a rational analysis of the resulting observations. A number of factors have been proposed by various authors as possible behavioral indicators that the individual may be manifesting demonic influence rather than (or in addition to) mental illness.

Table 5 presents a brief summary of the major behavioral indicators of demonic influence, culled from a number of sources. These are divided into two groups: Cultic or Occultic Religious Practices (elsewhere referred to as Avenues into the Demonic) and Other Clues. Avenues into the Demonic were discussed in an earlier chapter and are presented here in summary form only to complete the picture for diagnostic purposes.

The experience of Koch, Bubek, Dickason, and others has suggested that certain events and activities in personal history are probable indicators of demonic influence; they imply that these experiences are possible causes of demonic influence. These are included in the first group. In addition, several other behavioral features have been observed commonly among those who have been under demonic influence; these form the second group.[10]

A number of experiences are often found in association with demonic activity. There are two common themes: involvement in cultic or occultic religious practices, and habitual sinful activity, though not all the experiences fit neatly into these categories. These observations come from case studies and anecdotal evidence. All case-study data have definite limitations, such as selective attention and memory, overlooking of important aspects, attributing significance to very common events, and false causal inferences.[11]

Cultic and Occultic Practices   One indicator of possible demonic influence is a report that the individual has engaged in occultic religious practices. Another indicator is past or present involvement in an Eastern religion. Members of American Indian and Oriental ethnic groups also are more likely than those of other ethnic groups to manifest demonic influence. Common to all of these groups is spiritism; all involve worship

---

Behavioral Indicators of Possible Demonic Influence

A. Cultic or Occultic Religious Practices
   1. Involvement in the practice of magic.
   2. Involvement in occultic religious practices.
   3. Conscious invitation extended to Satan and/or demons to become involved in the person's life.
   4. Involvement in Eastern religions or ''New Age'' channeling practices.
   5. Family history of demonic influence, witchcraft, palmistry, Satanic worship, or other occult practices.
   6. History of living in areas without a strong Judeo-Christian cultural influence.
   7. Participation in American Indian or Oriental religious/cultural practices.
   8. Personal use of tarot cards, Ouija boards, horoscopes, palmistry, fortune tellers.

B. Other Clues
   1. Disinterest in or absence of spiritual growth by a professing Christian.
   2. Extreme negative reactions to the mention of God, Jesus Christ, the Holy Spirit, and to Christian religious practices.
   3. Systematic pattern of personal sinfulness.
   4. Prominent evidence of unforgiveness/bitterness and vengefulness.
   5. Unusually high resistance to benefits from medication and psychotherapy.
   6. Personality disturbance and especially multiple personality disorder (a dissociative disorder), rather than schizophrenia or psychosis.
   7. Addictive patterns such as abuse of alcohol or drugs, habitual gambling or sexual preoccupations.
   8. Personal preoccupation with power, position, wealth, and fame.

Table 5

---

of other than the living God: voodoo practices, ancestral shrines, and tribal religious practices, are examples of such worship. As we have seen, all false worship is ultimately worship of demons and their chief, Satan.[12] Thus, it should come as little surprise that such practices may result in demonic influence.

Personal use of tarot cards, horoscopes, Ouija boards, astrology, and visits to fortune tellers and soothsayers are also clues of potential demonic influence. Common to all of these activities is the desire to peek into the future, to know things that God has chosen not to reveal. Any search for supernatural knowledge that is not from God has potential for putting one in contact with the false god, Satan.

Perhaps surprising, but nonetheless an indicator according to several authors, is a history of having lived in countries where Christianity is not strong. Historically, North America has been influenced heavily by Christian values. Perhaps it is a mark of God's blessing that overt demonic influence has been relatively rare in this part of the world. However, with the increase of religious pluralism, it seems apparent that this is changing rapidly.

Another indicator of possible demonic influence in persons' lives is their having come from a family with a history of involvement in witchcraft, palmistry, occult practice, satanic worship, or overt demonic influence. Earlier it was stated that there is no biblical support for what Dickason and others term ancestral influence. However, we are warned in Scripture that God visits the sins of the fathers on the third and fourth generations of those who hate him (Exod. 20:1–6). Doubtless this occurs as they learn habits, attitudes, and behavior patterns that are passed from one generation to another.

The literature on cases of demonic influence suggests that persons may be dedicated to Satan at or before birth by their parents. This process parallels the Christian practice of dedicating children to the Lord. The initial perversion is that the parents commit themselves to teaching their children to engage in various cultic practices; the children, in turn, come under demonic influence through their own personal choices, which are at least partially in response to the influence of their parents or family.

Involvement in magical arts is a behavioral indicator that suggests possible demonic involvement.[13] Perhaps a more obvious indicator of demonic influence is the report of a direct, conscious invitation to Satan or demons. This is the "devil's pact" of literary renown and remains one of the strongest indicators of possible demonic influence.

Other Clues   Other clues of possible demonic influence, as suggested earlier, involve any life-dominating pattern of addiction or perversion. The well-known habits of abuse or addiction to alcohol, marijuana, heroin, cocaine, amphetamines, and other substances, whether licit or illicit, could provide an avenue into demonic influence. Similarly, other "addictive" habits such as compulsive gambling, masturbation or other sexual activities, overeating or undereating, and a host of others (perhaps even extreme obsessions with personal fitness or appearance) provide potential avenues into demonic influence.

The diagnostic problem with any of these patterns is the

ability to distinguish between sinful habits and demonic influence, especially possession. Certainly these habits can be enslaving, hence they may be a problem in their own right. Perhaps this is one way in which Satan's deceptiveness has enabled him to be effective in our time and culture, by working through the seemingly natural activities of a person's life style, developing one aspect into an idolatrous priority. Also, by working through "natural" means such as physical disease and mental disorder he is able to largely escape our notice.

We must remember that anything in a person's life that takes the place that properly belongs to the God of the universe is a false god, and thus inevitably opens the way for one to come under the influence of the god of this world. This could also be called idolatory. Again, the question we must often face is not *whether* Satan is involved, but *how.*

That sexual sins provide an avenue into demonic influence is suggested clearly in Scripture. Husbands and wives are reminded of their mutual obligations to each other sexually, and warned, "Stop depriving one another . . . lest Satan tempt you because of your lack of self-control" (1 Cor. 7:5).

Obsessive preoccupation with power, wealth, status, fame, influence, and popularity are also possible clues of demonic presence, because they too can become false gods. Most of us have heard stories of people who would do *anything,* so they tell their friends, to achieve some personal end.

Finally, and I believe central to all the other indicators of the demonic, is personal sin. Any systematic, habitual pattern of sin is a potential means of coming under demonic influence. We must be aware of the alliance and continuous interplay of the world, the flesh, and the devil. Central to all sin is a failure to love God fully and to submit ourselves to his divine will and guidance for our lives. To fail to submit is to side with Satan in adopting the view that we know better than God, and hence will decide for ourselves how to live our lives. Choosing Satan's side in the cosmic struggle between good and evil places us at risk of coming under the control of his demonic agents. Of course, those who are outside of a saving relationship with God through faith in Jesus Christ are already Satan's agents, hence under his influence in any event.

Other indicators of demonic influence include strong bitterness or unforgiveness of real or imagined transgressions suffered at the hands of others; this may be just a special case of habitual sin, since forgiveness is commanded by God. Extremely negative reactions to the mention of God, Jesus Christ, or the Holy Spirit, and to Christian religious practices also may be evidence of demonic influence.

The presence of personality disturbance rather than psychosis or schizophrenia (disorders which are likely to have strong biological roots) may suggest possible demonic influence. Multiple Personality in particular suggests possible demonic influence if Allison's view is correct. Allison, you may recall, is a psychiatrist who specializes in treatment of Multiple Personality Disorders. His approach to discerning the presence of demonic influence involves an evaluation of the characteristics of the "alter personalities" in people who manifest multiple personalities. He believes that true alter personalities always serve a consistent purpose for the individual, dealing consistently with the same unmanageable emotional condition. By contrast, he contends that demons are neither so predictable nor consistent. Finally, unusually high resistance to any benefit from medication may be an indicator of demonic influence according to some.

In examining for behavioral indicators of demonic influence a detailed personal history of the individual can be of great value. However, it is difficult at times to obtain the necessary information for a number of reasons. First, the individual may choose to withhold certain kinds of information to avoid embarrassment or risk. Second, the individual may overlook relevant information or discount its importance. Third, he or she may have forgotten or have never even known or recognized key events, especially if they occurred when the person was very young or if they involved activities of others, such as parents.

Two precautions are important in considering the significance of an individual's historical involvement in one of the avenues into demonic influence. The first is that the presence of any given historical event, or even several events, may not necessarily indicate demonic influence. There are doubtless many good Christians who have one or more of these experiences in their personal histories. While demonic influence is possible for such persons, many are likely to be relatively free from it. Similarly, the absence of these indicators does not completely eliminate the possibility of demonic influence. Nonetheless, a clear study of the individual's background for these indicators is one of the steps that should be taken in assessing the possibility of demonic influence.

The presence of even one of the behavioral indicators, with the possible exception of resistance to benefit from medication and counseling or psychotherapy, may be sufficient evidence to suggest some degree of demonic influence. It is significant that personal sinfulness is involved in most of the behavioral indicators. As we have seen from earlier chapters, personal sinfulness opens the door to demonic influence by providing an opportunity for Satan and his agents. Also, sin is, at its root, a choice against God; all such choices involve a commitment to the way of deception, and hence to the Deceiver himself.

In his study, Southard identifies three additional criteria which he considers to be behavioral. The first is "unusual feelings of apprehension and/or a sense of evil" in the presence of the individual. Second is "unusual behavior" such as tearing up a Bible, strange appearance or voice, attempts by the client to completely sabotage his or her health, and a vicious attitude toward self. A third sign suggested as evidence of demonic influence is psychological improvement during or after an exorcism.[14]

We have seen from our discussion above that unusual behavior is clearly included within the scope of mental illness. Thus, it seems doubtful that this criterion will be of much assistance in discerning the presence or absence of the demonic.

Similarly, evidence of improvement following exorcism is of dubious value. First, it seems quite possible that some persons will show temporary improvement following such an experience due simply to coincidental or "chance" factors related to the fluctuations of their condition over time. Attributing such changes to the effects of exorcism would clearly be erroneous. Worse, it could be harmful; if the person is misdiagnosed, the problem may reappear or even grow worse. Such worsening may be complicated by spiritual doubts arising out of the belief that exorcism has failed.

More seriously, there is abundant evidence in medical and psychological research literature supporting the conclusion that nonspecific effects of the treatment process (such as receiving attention, the concern of others, or the arousal of hope) result in improvement in many cases. This is known as the placebo effect.[15]

It cannot be said for certain that exorcism does not work. Still, some doubt remains that exorcism is effective from a scientific standpoint. So far, virtually all data on the effectiveness of exorcism come from case studies. Unfortunately, this means that there may be a number of competing explanations for any beneficial outcomes.[16]

Among these last three criteria proposed by Southard, we are left, then, with unusual feelings or the sense of the presence of evil. However, these are, in fact, intuitive rather than behavioral criteria. Thus they fall under the intuitive approach.

PROPOSED STRATEGY

Three approaches to diagnosing the presence of demonic influence have been suggested: discerning the spirits by means of intuition and the use of the spiritual gift of discernment, testing the spirits by directing them in the name and authority of Jesus to acknowledge their presence and state their name and rank, and behavioral observations and analysis of personal history. Although limited in their effectiveness, discerning the spirits and behavioral observations have merit.

Perhaps the best diagnostic strategy for counselors is to combine behavioral observations with intuition or spiritual discernment. In seeking to reach a conclusion about the nature of a particular person's problems, the helper would look for converging evidence from these two sources of information. When both point toward probable demonic influence, reasonable confidence can be placed in that conclusion. Similarly, where neither of those provides affirmative indications, demonic influence can be ruled out with some confidence.

This approach is consistent with that proposed by Michael Green. He recommends discernment, and the spiritual gift called "discernment of the spirits," as very helpful in recognizing whether a person is demonized. On one occasion, for example, upon entering a room in which a possessed person was standing, he noted, "I felt an immediate, almost palpable, sense of evil. . . ."[17] In addition, Green advocates diagnosis by means of a careful case history to discover whether important indicators are present. "One final word: if a person proclaims with great confidence that he is possessed, take leave to doubt it. The demons are normally in no hurry to invite expulsion."[18]

When discrepancies are found between indications from intuitive/spiritual discernment and behavioral factors, it is probably best to withhold judgment and proceed cautiously with intervention. Whatever the approach, take care to evaluate for the presence of additional problems, and seek further clarification of the diagnosis. The person receiving help should be informed of any uncertainty about the nature of his or her problem, and encouraged to help in the continuing diagnostic process.

Where discrepant evidence is found, the nature of the problem remains uncertain, and interventions require caution regardless of which direction the helper chooses. Naturally, in such instances the predilections of the helper are likely to be of major significance in determining the selected course of action; many pastors and lay Christian helpers may choose exorcism, while others, including many mental-health professionals, will more likely choose medication and counseling or psychotherapy approaches. As we shall see in the next two chapters, such ambiguity of diagnosis need not be a serious problem.

Essential Precautions

It has already been suggested that demonic influence may occur together with mental disorders. Further, we have seen that the task of clearly identifying the presence of demonic influence is at best uncertain. Thus, it is of great importance that steps be taken to rule out the presence of mental disorders and physical disorders. Though not widespread, stories exist of counselors who have provided counseling for seriously depressed individuals only to discover a brain tumor, hormonal deficiency, or other physical basis for the problem. Again, nothing is more futile than to "exorcise" or "deliver" a person afflicted with a tumor which has gone undetected. Similarly, while it may reduce some symptoms, no lasting benefit is likely to occur from treating a demon-possessed person with medication.

People are complex beings. There are complex interactions among the spiritual, psychological, and physical dimensions. Thus, even in the presence of clear indicators of a specific type of problem, such as demonic influence, it is by far the wisest course to obtain comprehensive medical, psychological, and spiritual evaluation, and to see that treatment is prescribed in each area of need.

SUMMARY

Three major approaches to discovering the presence of demonic influence have been developed. These involve the use of spiritual insight or the spiritual gift of "discerning the spirits," examination of personal history and behavioral indicators, and testing the spirits. The third approach is discounted as of dubious merit and without biblical support.

The approaches of spiritual discernment and examination of behavioral indicators both have some merit, though each is limited as well. Thus a prudent counselor will use elements of both and look for consistency in the conclusions drawn from the two approaches.

Because of the potential for interaction among the various dimensions of the person, there is a risk of overlooking problems in one or more areas. Thus, it is strongly advised that the person's spiritual, psychological, and physical functioning be carefully evaluated, and any needed treatment be given in each area. Usually, this will require referral to others, or a team approach. If these precautions are taken, it seems likely that an incorrect preliminary assessment of the person's status regarding demonic influence need not be a major problem. The next two chapters will develop this proposition in more detail.

CHAPTER TEN

SPIRITUAL INTERVENTIONS

In this chapter the focus is on some of the practical ways in which we may help our counselees prepare for and engage in spiritual warfare by making use of the protective resources God provides. As has been suggested throughout, in approaching counseling with those under demonic influence, it is important to remember that we function as psychophysical and spiritual wholes, and that there is continuous and complex interplay among the biological, social-emotional, and spiritual dimensions of the person.

As an organizational convenience, spiritual and nonspiritual interventions are presented in separate chapters. However, the ideal is that the two kinds of help occur together and move forward more or less simultaneously. In some circumstances, both forms of intervention, together with any needed medical help, may be provided to a substantial degree by one person, though my experience suggests that there are at least two benefits from working as a team.

First, it is very unusual for any one individual to have the range and degree of competence required to deal with all of the many facets of mental disorders and demonic influence, especially when the two are intertwined, as is sometimes the case. Second, the effectiveness of the intervention is greatly enhanced by combining the efforts of several people who work well together.

In this chapter we will examine spiritual warfare, explore methods for dealing with the sins of commission, address other spiritual interventions, and examine deliverance or casting out. More traditional counseling approaches will be examined in the next chapter.

SPIRITUAL WARFARE

The first approaches that come to mind for most believers in considering how to deal with demonic influence are those of deliverance, casting out, or exorcism. It is important to recognize that there is no biblically prescribed pattern for exorcism. It is true that a number of biblical examples may be cited of the casting out of demons. Most of these, as we have seen in chapter 3, occurred during the life of Christ, and the remaining instances occurred during the apostolic era.

The fact that the Scriptures lack specific instruction regarding the practice of exorcism, or the casting out of demons, presents us with a bit of a dilemma. First, we must beware of adopting any narrowly prescribed approach. And second, we must begin with those things that are clearly taught in Scripture. Only when we have done what God clearly commands, and have ceased doing what God clearly forbids, ought we to consider doing things about which the Scripture does not speak. We must consider these latter things—about which the Bible is silent—as matters of judgment in any event.

Since the Bible is silent about procedures for exorcism, we will begin with the clear commandments and prohibitions regarding how we are to deal with demonic influence. Later we will return to the question of exorcism.

The basic biblical teachings regarding the believer's means of becoming free from demonic influence involve seven aspects which commence following the new creation.

1. considering ourselves dead to sin;
2. being filled with the Holy Spirit;
3. fleeing from temptation;
4. submitting ourselves to God as instruments of righteousness;
5. practicing righteousness;
6. regular, ongoing confession of sin;
7. resisting Satan and his demons by the power of our testimony and with the armor of God.[1]

In contrast to the absence of biblical instruction regarding exorcism or deliverance, numerous Scripture passages address the above matters. We are instructed: "Submit therefore to God. Resist the devil and he will flee from you. Draw near to God and He will draw near to you" (James 4:7–8). We are to "put on the full armor of God, that [we] may be able to stand firm against the schemes of the devil" (Eph. 6:11). Having been freed from sin, we are to become slaves to righteousness, knowing that God has called us to such and that the result is beneficial in sanctification and eternal reward (Rom. 6:11–22).

These basic instructions are repeated throughout the New Testament epistles: submit to God, resist the devil, and use the resources God provides for the life we are to live as believers. In his high priestly prayer just before his crucifixion, Christ prayed that his disciples would be protected from the evil one (John 17:15). This prayer was not only for the disciples, but for all believers (John 17:20). Thus, God's goal appears to be to protect us through the means outlined above, rather than to remove us from the world, which is the sphere of Satan's influence.

Submit and Resist The first step in the process of becoming free from demonic influence involves submission to God and resistance to Satan. For the unbeliever, this means, first of all, acknowledging his or her sinfulness and receiving God's salvation. Since the unbeliever belongs to Satan's kingdom, he or she cannot expect to be free from demonic influence apart from this radical change of allegiance. For the believer, such a change of kingdoms is not necessary, but believers must nonetheless repent, confess, and seek the filling of the Holy Spirit as they choose to commit their ways to God (i.e., as they submit to God).

As Scripture repeatedly illustrates, this process of submission to God is not easily accomplished. Both the Old and New Testament historical accounts are filled with examples, several of which were presented earlier (see chapter 3). Nonetheless, submission to God is the first step toward freedom from demonic influence.

The Armor of God In Ephesians, Paul presents a brief summary of the resources that God has provided for us in our struggle against satanic and demonic influence. In his description of the armor of God, Paul draws a parallel between the equipment of a soldier prepared for battle and the equipment of the believer for spiritual warfare (Eph. 6:12–17).

A careful study of Ephesians 6 will be of great value in preparing to deal with demonic influence. Here we can only outline the major elements.

First, we notice that the warfare is spiritual, thus the equipment must be spiritual. Its employment enables us to resist and to stand firm.

We are to wrap ourselves with the truth, put on the breastplate of righteousness, cover our feet with the gospel of peace, take up the shield of faith, wear the helmet of salvation, and take up the sword of the Spirit, the Word of God. It is noteworthy that the major elements of this warfare are defensive, with one exception, the Word of God.

Notice again the armor: truth, righteousness, peace, faith, salvation, and the Word of God. In appropriating the armor of God we must begin with these. I'm tempted to say that we begin with one, adding others one by one. But it is not so simple. Salvation is not possible apart from a knowledge of and faith in the truth; the moment salvation is taken up it begins to produce righteousness and peace with God. Thus, these qualities, these pieces of armor, cannot ultimately be thought of as separate elements from which we may pick and choose those we would use on a given occasion. Rather, there is an intimate interconnectedness among them; we must appropriate all of them if we are to be protected effectively from demonic influence; the alternative is to risk more serious demonic influence (see Luke 11:24–28).

Slavery to Righteousness It is not enough for demons to be cast out of a person. Something has to take their place before he or she can be assured of ongoing freedom from demonic influence (see chapter 3).

The process of becoming free from demonic influence requires developing new patterns of living which replace the old sinful patterns associated with demonic influence. This involves spiritual growth, and the discipline of righteousness. The Bible speaks of this process as that of becoming slaves (or servants) to righteousness.

This transformation from sinful to godly patterns of living takes time. Only through the repeated experience of testing and trial are we able to cultivate the specific pattern of righteousness we need, or develop more fundamental traits of patience, hope, endurance, and the love of God, which characterize maturity (Rom. 5:1–5; James 1:2–4).

There is a bit of a paradox here. Human freedom is not freedom in an absolute sense. Rather, it is freedom from the penalty, power, and presence of sin, freedom to respond as servants to God. It is to this freedom, and only to this freedom, that those enslaved by demonic influence may be delivered.[2]

PRACTICAL APPLICATION

The counselee needs to personally receive Christ if he or she is not a believer. As we have earlier said, if not a Christian, the person belongs to the kingdom of Satan. This has two major practical implications. First, the person may not desire to change, and second, even if the desire is present, without the presence of the Holy Spirit he or she may lack the necessary spiritual resources to make the needed changes.

The counselee needs to be active. He or she must confess and renounce all sin and occultic involvement; all objects or connections with the spirit world must be removed and, preferably, destroyed (see Acts 8:9–25). Satan and demons must be actively resisted. Conscious commitment to Christ and to following the commands of Scripture should be reflected in reading and memorizing Scripture, praying for personal growth and deliverance, participating in Christian fellowship, serving in whatever capacity is suitable, and in sharing the gospel. He or she should solicit prayer from understanding fellow-believers.

Two major dimensions underlie this activity. First, the person must actively bring his or her will, attitudes, and personal conduct into conformity with the commandments of God, thus carrying out the injunction "submit therefore to God."

Second, there must be a practical outworking of the instruction to "resist the devil." This involves forsaking former companions and haunts, diligently changing habits from sinful patterns to godly ones—especially in the most needful areas—laying aside the old self and putting on the new self, which is in the likeness of God (see Eph. 4:22–24). In particular, any known sinful habit must be confessed and renounced. Any repetitive sinful pattern, as we have noted, provides an avenue for invasion by the demonic for influence or control.

While God is able to remove old patterns of behavior and old attitudes instantly, he does not normally do so. Rather, he calls us to work out our own salvation in this regard, while he graciously motivates us and gives us the power to change through the Holy Spirit (see Philippians 2:12–13). Just as God allowed the nation of Israel to conquer the land of Canaan bit by bit, so he allows us to gradually gain control over ungodly patterns of living in a progressive fashion. These old patterns of sinful thoughts and behavior are like a part of "Canaan" still held by the enemy. Only through the consistent practice of godliness do we gain complete freedom from demonic influence in these areas of our lives. The same is true for counselees. As Dickason notes, "Practicing these things will assure growth and deliverance from the enemy at the proper time."[3]

Be aware that just as submission to God is a process that may vary in terms of degree, so resistance to Satan may vary in degree, and deliverance may also be a matter of degree.[4] In his high-priestly prayer, Jesus did not pray that God would remove his followers from the world, but that God would protect them from "the evil one" (John 17:15). In a sense then, while this life lasts, all protection is a matter of degree, that is, the degree to which we cooperate with God.

Since the transformation toward righteousness is not instantaneous, absolute, or accomplished in isolation, the counselee needs to be involved in a supportive community, in fellowship, individual and corporate prayer, Bible study, worship, and service to others. Counseling from professionals may be needed, and will be much more effective if it occurs along with this process of spiritual transformation.

SINS OF COMMISSION

Many of the avenues into demonic influence involve the commission of overt sinful actions. Due to the limitations of space, we will only be able to present illustrative examples of these patterns here. The New Testament is replete with instructions to cease practices that are sinful and ungodly. Many of these commands are followed by directives to initiate an alternative pattern, thus moving in the opposite direction. This is the essence of repentance.

The practice of repentance is a key to the elimination of many problematic behavior patterns that contribute to demonic influence. Repentance carries with it the notion of making an about-face and proceeding in the opposite direction. We are told, "Let him who steals steal no longer; but rather let him labor, performing with his own hand what is good, in order that he may have something to share with him who has need" (Eph. 4:28). As Adams puts it, "When is a thief not a thief? When he works and gives." Otherwise, he is merely a thief on vacation.

The degree of demonic influence may be small or great; the sinful pattern associated with demonic influence may be subtle or overt. But the pattern the Bible prescribes for freedom always involves repentance.

Cindy Cindy was a woman in her early forties, married over twenty years, with two teen-age boys. Her husband was emotionally aloof, but critical, somewhat like her father. Cindy suffered from low self-esteem, and found this unsupportive relationship very painful. She first came to me complaining of a chronic and moderately severe depression. As I came to know

155

Cindy, I discovered that over the years she had begun to seek affection and encouragement outside the marriage relationship, entering into several affairs.

At the time Cindy came to see me she had been involved for a couple of years with a former high-school boyfriend who was now three times divorced. She had broken up with him during high school because her father insisted that Larry was no good. Her depression stemmed from at least three factors: self-esteem problems, guilt, and conflict which developed with Larry as she began to discover that he was lying to her and probably involved in relationships with other women as well.

The extent of demonic involvement in Cindy's problems was probably moderate. It was not an issue that either she or I identified in the counseling relationship. Yet we both recognized that what she was doing was wrong, and that it needed to change. She had believed the satanic lie that the only way to happiness was by means of a more satisfying relationship with a man, even though that man was not her husband. Having begun the pattern of involvement, she was entangled in a steadily worsening cycle of transgression, guilt, exploitation by Larry, and discouragement deepening into depression. As a result, she felt the desperate need for Larry even more keenly. Only in retrospect did Cindy come to believe that adultery, the solution that she had chosen, not only failed to cure her self-esteem problems, it made things worse.

For Cindy to become free from this pattern, it was not enough to stop seeing Larry, though that was one step. She also needed to begin to seek social-emotional relationships and intimacy in other ways, especially to seek reconciliation with her husband. Only by becoming a servant to righteousness could this woman become free from slavery to sin and begin to develop a healthy view of herself.

Numerous other examples of sinful patterns are given in the last three chapters of Ephesians, and throughout the New Testament Epistles. We are to cease lying, bitterness (being unforgiving), filthy talk, outbursts of anger, sexual immorality, gluttony, gossip, covetousness, idolatry, drunkenness, malice, selfishness, pride, disobedience to authority figures, seeking to please men rather than God, anxious worry, and a host of other sinful patterns.

The Bible suggests a variety of approaches that one might use in helping counselees give up sinful patterns. The particular one chosen must be fitted to the needs of the individual. Counselees may need to be taught the Word, to be encouraged, exhorted, reproved, rebuked. At times, witnesses may need to be brought into the situation. At other times the person may need to be brought before the church and even to be removed from the church body and treated as an unbeliever. These latter two approaches rarely fall within the role of the counselor, and may even be unethical under the normal confidentiality agreements of counseling. However, they are tools that need to be used in our churches and personal relationships when appropriate.[5]

Most often, those who come seeking counseling on their own initiative need to be approached gently. Although they may recognize that they are involved in sin, and experience considerable guilt, they nonetheless seem to be caught in an inextricable web. The web may be of their own making, yet they need help in escaping.

There are four important dimensions to the problems of such individuals: thoughts, behavior, emotions, and relationships.

1. Thoughts. Part of Satan's character is that he lies; this is one aspect of demonic influence that is both subtle and pervasive. As C. S. Lewis suggests, blatant lies do not succeed in deceiving most people; rather, truth with a twist is what Satan uses. Thus, a first step in freeing people from demonic influence in this regard is to help them comprehend the truth and recognize the lies they hear from others, or all too often tell themselves (see Jeremiah 17:9).

In this process of moving from lies to truth, the use of Scripture is of great value. Often I ask a person to go home and read a chosen passage of Scripture daily, even several times a day, for a week or more. I may also instruct the person to record thoughts, feelings, and reactions to this reading. Memorizing and pondering (meditating on) Scripture is of even greater benefit, though it is harder to get cooperation with this more difficult task.

At other times, a line or phrase may be quoted with great benefit. One of my colleagues, when confronted with people who face the dilemma of unpleasant events that are beyond their control, listens to them tell of their fears. He then encourages them to accept what they must face, concluding with, "Sometimes all you can say is 'Thy will be done.'"

The approach of Larry Crabb is somewhat similar to this. The first step Crabb advocates is transformation of thinking, through learning and applying biblical truth. In Crabb's model, the transformation of behavior and feelings follows transformation of thought.[6] This approach is especially helpful with bright verbal people who have a reasonably good understanding of their own functioning. For others, however, the approaches which follow may be more effective.

2. *Behavior.* Problem habits (or behaviors) are often inextricably linked with thoughts and beliefs. God made us to be creatures of habit; that is both a strength and a problem. Without habits it would take forever to get dressed in the morning. Habits serve us well, but also cause great difficulty. Habits enable us to carry out routine tasks quickly and efficiently, with little thought. They are hard to form, and also hard to eradicate. More significantly, habits are easier to replace than to merely discard.

The nightly habit of going to the tavern and drinking is not easily eliminated by a person's determining to stop going to the tavern. Usually, such a person skips a night or two, perhaps even several, then resumes drinking more strongly than ever. This pattern may be eradicated more successfully if replaced by another activity, e.g., attending AA meetings on a nightly basis. Other new habits may also work to eliminate the custom of drinking at the tavern, provided they replace (compete with) the tavern-drinking pattern effectively.[7]

It may seem surprising to some, but it is often easier to change thoughts through changing behavior than it is to change behavior through changing one's thoughts. For example, a person is more likely to adopt an antiabortion view if he or she is asked to develop a talk arguing against abortion than if required to listen to antiabortion lectures.[8]

Tammy Tammy was a young woman who came for counseling at her husband's encouragement because of a compulsive spending problem. She had an indulgent mother for whom money was never a problem, and had developed the view that she could always get anything she wanted. She also was lonely, isolated from family, and uninvolved in church activities because of a recent move. As a result, she had become depressed. Her way of coping with the emotional poverty of her life was to buy things, especially clothes.

Tammy's spending was a definite problem, and had resulted in considerable debt. However, it quickly became apparent that to deal effectively with her compulsive spending, it would be necessary to address the underlying depression, loneliness, and frustration. For the buying sprees to be eliminated, Tammy needed to develop new relationships that replaced those she had given up for the move.

She recognized that her spending was a problem, and was motivated to change, but seemed incapable. My task was to help her constructively focus her efforts on the larger problem, of which she was almost completely ignorant. Thus, almost paradoxically, though her buying sprees were the initial focus, exploring the factors that prompted them led us to her problem emotions of loneliness and depression. Only when these emotional roots were clear was it possible to identify the need to develop satisfying relationships as the solution. Changing her lonely, isolating behavior led to changed thoughts and feelings about spending money, resulting in changed spending habits.

3. *Emotions.* As we have just seen, thoughts and behaviors are linked to emotions in an intricate manner. In dealing with emotions, the first thing we often need to do is face the truth regarding emotions. Sadly, in some churches emotions are treated as if they are at best trivial consequences of thought and action, or even something to be avoided as if a curse. The truth of the matter is far different. Emotions may be either good or bad, depending on how we use them, just as is true for the rest of God's creation.

In understanding emotions, we must begin with some basic facts. First, God himself is portrayed as emotional (see Deuteronomy 9:7–8, 19–20). Second, God made us to be emotional creatures (see Genesis 1:26–27). Third, when God finished the Creation, he pronounced it good (Gen. 1:31). Fourth, we are instructed at numerous points in Scripture to experience certain emotions: to mourn and to be miserable, to rejoice, to celebrate, to encourage and be encouraged, to be joyful (for example, see Joel 2:12; Philippians 4:4; James 4:9).

Emotions are a God-given resource.[9] The problem emotions, such as anger, fear, and anxiety, are like the warning lights on the dashboard of a car. They warn that something is wrong; failure to heed the warning may result in serious problems. Conversely, the pleasant emotions are a signal that things are going well. Naturally, false signals can be received. People may feel guilty when they have not transgressed (even so, the emotion may serve a useful warning function). Thus we do well to examine our emotions and their sources; we ignore them at our peril.

Another problem emotion is doubt. Habermas points out that doubt is multifaceted; it may be cognitive-intellectual, volitional-behavioral, or emotional in nature, or it may. be a complex combination of two or more types. Emotional doubt is exhibited, for example, when persons profess to know that God loves them and has forgiven them, but they just don't feel God's love and forgiveness. Such doubt may pose a serious problem for the life of a believer.

For a person who experiences emotional doubt, it is often helpful to begin with a review of the facts of his or her relationship to God and with biblical teachings which indicate that God's forgiveness is certain and that he will not refuse any who come to him in repentance (for example, John 6:37). Frequent reminders of these facts may go a long way toward dispelling doubt.

In addition to reviewing biblical reassurances, the person needs to be encouraged to begin practicing those things that God calls him or her to do. The possibilities are numerous, but can be briefly summarized as loving God and loving one's neighbor. There is nothing quite like performing practical deeds of love to dispel doubts about forgiveness (see 1 John 3:14–24).

One emotion which I believe is too much neglected is that of joy. I find nothing in Scripture that encourages us to seek happiness, though happiness seems to be a common human pursuit.

The "pursuit of happiness" is even addressed in the U.S. Constitution. However, the kingdom of God is "righteousness, peace, and joy . . ." (Rom. 14:17). A question which I have found helpful personally and with counselees is "what brings you joy?" When I ask that of myself, the answer is far different from the answer to what makes me happy. I may be happy when I walk on the beach, or when I finish a good game of racquetball, or when I've had a few hours away from work.

What brings me joy is another matter. It is confronting a student with serious problems in his or her preparation, proposing needed remediation, and warning that an unsatisfactory grade or even dismissal may occur if such steps are not taken, and then finding that the counsel has been heeded, and the problems addressed.

Tears of joy came to my eyes the day I discovered my daughter, then about two and a half years old, poised at the end of the driveway, watching her friends disappear into the backyard across the street. She was left there alone because she had obeyed my instruction that she was not to go into the street. I could continue with other examples. What links them is doing right in difficult situations and helping others to do so. Joy is a fruit of the Holy Spirit, experienced when we are in a harmonious relationship with God. What brings you joy?

The traditional Hebrew greeting, Shalom, is at once a blessing, a greeting, and a wish for a pleasant emotional condition much like that of joy. It is difficult to define briefly. In summary, it is a wish that the person so greeted would experience a comprehensive sense of peace, health, and well-being in the physical, mental, social, and spiritual dimensions. To cultivate Shalom and be involved in all those activities that bring it about is to move in the direction of joy; that direction is diametrically opposite to that which brings one under demonic influence.

As noted earlier, overt demonic influence (or possession) is not the only way Satan and his agents work. Satan's work is not only more often subtle than overt, it is also more common and widespread than is generally believed. While demon possession may simulate mental disorders, and may occur together with them, this is likely to be the exception rather than the rule. Thus, those who are demon possessed are not likely to show up very often in the offices of pastors, Christian counselors, psychologists, psychiatrists, and other mental health workers. Nonetheless, the counselor often deals with those who experience more limited degrees of demonic influence. He or she must be prepared to recognize and deal with those whose lives are affected by persons who are under demonic influence or are possessed.

Scott Peck, in his book *People of the Lie,* suggests that in his experience "truly evil people" tend to be family members of those whom he sees rather than persons who seek therapy for themselves. Often these truly evil people appear to be strikingly successful in a variety of ways. Yet, behind the scenes, someone is paying the price for their evil. It is their victims, often family members, who manifest mental disorders. Such has been my experience as well, as the following cases illustrate.

Angela   Angela was a fourteen-year-old junior-high student when she was first seen for counseling. The presenting complaint was that she was in constant conflict with her mother; she had begun to run away, and to express suicidal impulses. Though she was quite desperate, Angela was also reluctant to participate in counseling. She complained repeatedly that it was her mother who was the problem, explaining that Mom would become capriciously hostile with her and would physically abuse her; she would make promises to her and then break them. Thus Angela was constantly angry with her mother.

At one point Angela ran away from home, refusing to return or to let her parents know where she was, though she called the counselor to relay to her parents the message that she was safe. Tentative arrangements for her return home were negotiated, but broke down. The condition her parents required was that Angela firmly promise to stop provoking her mother. But Angela declined, claiming that nothing she could do would prevent her mother's rage.

During this period Angela's father was seen alone. When confronted about Angela's view, he readily agreed that his wife had a serious problem, but indicated that he was committed to taking his wife's side in any disagreement between her and Angela.

Eventually Angela returned home, but things continued to be very chaotic. It became clear from continued work with the parents that Angela's mother was a closet alcoholic and her raging outbursts occurred when she had been drinking. Angela doubtless provided minor provocations to her mother, but her mother's responses were highly unpredictable since Angela did not know when she had been drinking.

Sadly, Angela received limited help, though she was able to be somewhat more effective in avoiding provocation of her mother. She also became less suicidal as she gained some support in affirming that she was not "crazy."

In this case, while Angela was by no means innocent, the real evil lay with her parents. Her mother was an alcoholic who chose not to face her drinking problem. And her father was unwilling to risk his wife's hostility even to protect Angela from the injustice of her mother's outbursts of rage.

Jill Jill was first seen for counseling as an adult in her midtwenties. She had graduated from college, and was working as an accounts clerk, a job that was probably well within her abilities. An only child who lived with her parents, she came complaining of depression and difficulty handling her work responsibilities. The initial phases of counseling were extremely difficult, particularly because this woman was almost uncommunicative despite her professed desire for help. In the early weeks Jill reported that she had been sexually assaulted on a date while in college; later she had been sexually exploited by a male passenger in the adjoining seat while on a lengthy bus trip (in DSM-III-R this man's behavior might be diagnosed as Frotteurism). In each case Jill had told no one.

After several months of extremely slow progress, this woman continued to have difficulty performing her work, was very depressed, and had occasional suicidal thoughts. Eventually it was revealed that she had been sexually abused by her father. Jill's father had explained his behavior by telling Jill that some fathers had a "special love" for their daughters, and that that was the nature of his relationship with her. Following this discovery, she was encouraged to move from her parents' home, which she had done.

Several months later, it was learned that the sexual abuse by her father was still ongoing, though at much reduced frequency. A major breakthrough came when Jill confronted her father, telling him that she loved him, but that this was not an acceptable way to express it; she let him know that she would call the authorities and press charges if it occurred again.

Subsequently, it was learned that Jill's father had sought her for sexual purposes following conflict between him and her mother; thus, there was an element of overt hostility in his sexual relationship with her. Though Jill had come to perceive this relationship as exploitive, it is doubtful that she ever recognized the veiled anger in her father's actions. It is difficult to be certain, but it is suspected that her mother knew about her father's sexual exploitation, but chose not to confront him with it because then she would have had to deal with his anger. While other factors were involved, a major part of Jill's difficulties was the result of the sin of others.

4. Relationships. Since human evil most commonly involves relationships with other persons, it is important to address not only the thoughts, feelings, and behavior, but also the relational aspects of personal difficulties. Also, since God is a person, our interaction with him is relational; most fundamentally, sin affects our relationship with God.

The problems of Cindy, described earlier, were also problems of relationships: a critical, fault-finding father and an uncommunicative husband. Because she did not find emotional closeness in relationship with them, Cindy spent years seeking it in other relationships.

So then, thoughts, feelings, behavior, and relationships all are important. A common error is to focus on one or another of these dimensions and to largely neglect the others. Yet Scripture clearly teaches that it is important to deal with all of these dimensions of personal functioning. The commandments to love God and our neighbor are comprehensive commandments that involve the whole person: "You shall love the Lord your God with all your heart, and with all your soul, and with all your mind" (Matt. 22:37). Entering into relationships is central to love.

Much of the work of counselors involves teaching counselees how to deal with relationships and with the evil of those around them. We need also to teach people how to protect themselves so that they experience God's mercy rather than the more predictable outcome of "the sins of the fathers"—evil results that carry down to the third and fourth generation (see Exod. 20:5–6).

When the opportunity presents itself, it may also be possible to deal directly with those who are evil by working with the spouses or parents, or with others involved in the lives of counselees who are troubled. Such opportunities are more often afforded to pastors and laypersons within the church than to professional counselors since pastors and lay counselors are much more likely to know the families of those who are experiencing chronic depression, low self-esteem, and other mental disorders that are the result of being victimized.

OTHER SPIRITUAL INTERVENTIONS

To free a person from demonic influence, one vital aspect of spiritual intervention involves encouraging the individual to become actively involved in a local church body. This is a natural next step for new believers. For those who are believers, and thus may already be a part of a church community, it may be necessary to encourage more active personal involvement.

Our relationship with God also involves relationships with others. The second great commandment is to love others as we love ourselves. This requires association with them in an intimate and comprehensive manner. Sadly, in our individualistic culture we tend to neglect this interconnected or corporate aspect of faith which is ours in the body of Christ. Unfortunately, this results in many persons' being isolated from the healing capacity of relationships.

Several aspects of local church involvement are vital. First, this is a natural way to begin the process of mental transformation from an ungodly to a godly viewpoint. Second, it is in such community life that true purpose and meaning in life may be found. Third, churches provide a natural context for involvement in meaningful support groups, especially when the church fosters small-group fellowship and study. Fourth, the humble and gentle practice of church discipline may support the transformation that is needed. Finally, the local church is a natural context for deeds of practical service to God and fellow humans.[10]

The only true basis for meaning and purpose in life is a saving relationship with the God of Creation. For this relationship to grow and mature, it must be nurtured in the context of the local church. However, we live in an age of spiritual orphans; "baby" Christians may be related to their "spiritual parents" for only a brief period of time before a move, a job change, or personal choice separates them. It seems little wonder that many starve and some are snatched away by the evil one. Involvement in a local church family where the Bible is taught and practiced is a necessary part of the effort to grow up into maturity, and thereby become free from demonic influence.

Support Groups

In this day of mega-churches, it is easy for the individual to become anonymous and uninvolved. Small groups within the church are one effective way of minimizing this problem. Placing a counselee in a group of people who worship, study, pray, and minister together and to each other is one of the most helpful interventions I have found. This is true both for those with mental disorders and demonic influence. God's method for healing is through people who are his representatives.

A key dimension of support groups is fellowship, sharing in the lives of others. In this context many of the other spiritual processes important to spiritual and emotional healing occur naturally. In such groups one can experience corporate prayer, group Bible study, mutual encouragement, exhortation, service, and even practical discipline.

Prayer

Entering into communication with God, both on an individual and a corporate basis is a vital part of the healing process for those who struggle with demonic influence. However, certain safeguards are essential. It is quite possible for a person to actively contemplate and plan his or her next transgression while supposedly confessing past sins to God. Therefore, prayers of confession should be candid and brief. These ought not to become the central point of one's prayer life. It is significant that in the model prayer which Jesus taught, one moves from confession of sins to granting forgiveness to those who have sinned against one.

Many additional matters of prayer are called to our attention in this brief model prayer. The focus is not only on our own needs for forgiveness and daily care, but on the needs of others. Another important focus is on exalting God and submitting to his headship, bringing our motives into conformity with his wishes. Consequently, we come before God and invite him to search our hearts and reveal wicked motives, and then guide us into pure ones.

Paula   Paula provides a practical example of intervention in which prayer was used. This woman came to see me because of discouragement. She had been unable to work for over two years due to a degenerative disease, but had only recently learned its true nature and that its effects were not reversible; she experienced chronic pain, deteriorated mental functioning, and reduced energy. She expressed the desire to serve God during what remained of her life, but seemed unable to see any way in which she could serve. Paula also struggled with chronic guilt feelings regarding past sins, and the fear that God was punishing her for them.

As we explored her concerns, Paula's desire to serve God seemed genuine. She reported that she had confessed her former sins, and knew that God had forgiven her, but she still had nagging guilt feelings. She also reported that she had lost her self-esteem. It seemed that she had formerly derived much of her satisfaction in life from her job, which required intensive involvement with people, but now she was isolated and missed the social interaction and support.

As we explored what Paula could do now, I suggested that she consider discussing this with her pastor, and that she begin to pray that God would show her someone who needed her. During the next week she spoke with her pastor, but came away feeling that he was not very encouraging. He had suggested that she write a letter to the elder board describing her circumstances and expressing her desire. Seeing that she seemed reluctant to do so, I sought to encourage her.

The next week Paula reported that she had decided not to write the letter to the elders. She wasn't sure that it would be helpful, and she was aware that she probably had not recently been manifesting the quality of spiritual life that would inspire confidence in her ability to minister to others. Because she had been experiencing considerable grief regarding her poor health, she was in need of support and encouragement herself. I encouraged her to continue to pray that God would show her someone who needed her. She agreed.

The next time I saw Paula she reported having talked with her sixteen-year-old son from a former marriage, who had just made an unsuccessful suicide attempt and was quite depressed. The boy had left Paula's home and had gone to live with his father in another state about three years earlier because of conflict with Paula's second husband. Things had become so bad then that some physical abuse had occurred and threats of more harm had been made. In the interim, however, forgiveness and healing had taken place and the new husband had shown definite spiritual growth. Now the son was asking if he could once more live with Paula and his stepfather.

As we reflected on this, it was not clear that an immediate move was wise. Perhaps the boy could return to his mother later, after the school year had ended. Regardless, it was clear that he needed her. God had given Paula a person to whom she could minister! It seemed providential that he was one of the persons about whom she felt the most guilt for her past failures that had permitted the abusive interaction to occur.

Though it is doubtful that any individual in this family is demon possessed, there are clear patterns of sin involving each family member as they have interacted with the others. Satan has been successful in undermining this woman's effectiveness as a spiritual guide to her son in the past. Just as clearly, Paula's prayer for God's guidance in finding ways to show his love to others had produced a change in and for Paula.

Worship

The worship of God is another important aspect of spiritual intervention. Anyone who desires to become free from demonic influence must regularly worship (acknowledging God's worth), both individually and corporately. Jesus warned in a parable that a house that had been swept free of evil influence must be filled with good; worship of God is one aspect of that good.

Worship can, and should, take both individual and corporate forms. The settings may be quite varied: in a church, in one's home, on the beach or in the woods, even in one's car on the way to work. What is essential to worship is the conscious acknowledgment and expression of God's qualities—patience, mercy, justice, goodness, and others. The methods also are varied.[11]

Use of Scripture

Scripture is God's guidebook for living, as it reveals the truth that is essential to spiritual freedom. Reading, studying, memorizing, and meditating upon Scripture is another essential element of spiritual intervention for those who desire freedom from demonic influence. Sadly, all too few are willing to spend even a few minutes a day in such activities. Yet we are told that God's Word is the light for our way, the means of cleansing, a resource for the renewal of our minds. While not every person can reach the same level of biblical knowledge, all can become actively involved in seeking to know God's thoughts, words and ways. It is especially through memorizing and meditating that God's Word speaks to us, enlightens us, and guides us at crucial moments in our lives.

The Practice of Godly Living

Knowledge of Scripture is not enough in itself; it must be practiced. Indeed, there is much in Scripture that suggests that if we are to know it, we must come to know it through experience so that our comprehension is broadened by our actions and deepened by our experience of God's faithfulness as we respond in obedience to him.

Such disciplines as loving those close to us as we love ourselves, regarding their concerns as paramount, respecting their opinions as highly as our own, and giving them first place rather than ourselves, have a dual effect. By our obedience we are drawing closer to God; and his promise is that as we draw close to him he will draw near to us. Like any other human faculty, this aspect of faith grows strong only when it is exercised regularly. Put differently, godly living is the exercise of living faith.

Many of the spiritual interventions presented in this section are actually aspects of such living faith.

Spiritual Giving

Another dimension of becoming free from demonic influence involves the faithful, regular practice of returning to God's use a portion of his material blessing to us. It is widely agreed that the tithe, literally 10 percent, is a good guideline for giving; some may be able to give far more while others may, because of limited resources, sacrifice even to give less. Freedom from demonic influence involves such regular giving.

Jesus said that our hearts are in the same place as our treasure. Again and again experience shows that our efforts and attention are focused where we make monetary investment. Such a focus reduces focus on self or on the demonic. It is not possible to serve God and mammon (see Matthew 6:24).

Service

As was suggested earlier, in our discussion of doubt, practical deeds of loving service to others are among the most fundamental of God's commandments. Service is also one of the major elements of dealing with demonic influence. The person who would be free from such influence needs to be encouraged to begin serving in whatever capacity he or she is initially able. No task, when done in service to God, is without its reward (Matt. 10:42). Moreover, such service is a part of the process of submission to God and resistance to Satan.

Church Discipline

It is unfortunate that we live in a day in which church discipline is seldom practiced. As a result, petty sins or minor failures tend to become established habit patterns. The problem could be gossip, pride, haughtiness (lack of submission), or a host of other sinful patterns. When unchecked, these result in openness to demonic influence on the part of those who practice them. As noted above, often those who are around such individuals suffer most. But the individual also suffers.

George George's problem was pride. He was highly capable and intelligent, but because of pride found it difficult to get along with others. As a consequence, in his work George was frequently passed over, and others of lesser abilities were promoted. This resulted in bitterness and many job changes for George.

At the same time, members of his family suffered because George had little tolerance for even the smallest imperfection among them. The problem was sufficiently obvious that one wonders that the leaders of the churches which George attended seemed not to have addressed it. Perhaps prayerful encouragement, remonstrance, rebuke—that is, church discipline—might have had beneficial effect, particularly since George was quite concerned that he be regarded as an outstanding Christian.

The practice of church discipline may also be an important factor in dealing with those who habitually neglect or abuse people around them. I have observed a few occasions when such discipline has been exercised with good effect.

CASTING OUT AND EXORCISM

By this point, it should be clear that the practices of casting out demons and exorcism are not generally the preferred approach in dealing with demonic influence. Rather, one begins with submission to God and resisting the devil; one takes advantage of the whole armor of God, and disciplines oneself to godliness through the practice of righteous deeds.

However, as in alcohol and drug abuse an individual can reach the point where the ability to make meaningful choices is so clouded that he or she can no longer realistically consider changing, so persons who are demon possessed may have diminished capacity for meaningful choices.

In demon possession, the individual may be so strongly influenced by the demon that he or she is unable to think clearly or make an independent decision. The demon is quite readily able to maintain control, and thus to effectively block the person's efforts to break free.

In such extremes, exorcism or the casting out of demons seems most appropriate. At this point Dickason makes the observation that while the Bible does not advocate exorcism, it likewise does not forbid it. Before we address this process, however, one clarification is needed.

Michael Green draws what he considers to be an important distinction between exorcism and deliverance. Exorcism in Roman Catholic theology is reserved for those who are so dominated by demons that they are no longer able to exercise their own decision-making capacity.

> This rare and extreme situation may only be handled by priests specially authorized by the local bishop. The Church of Rome requires that such exorcism be done in the name of and with the authority of the church.[12]

By contrast, "deliverance" for the relief of believing Christians may be practiced by priest and laity alike. In deliverance, Green recommends a simple formula: "In the name of Jesus Christ, unholy spirit, I command you to depart from this creature of God."[13]

The distinction which Green draws appears to have both validity and value. In simpler cases, involving minor degrees of demonic influence, the personal disciplines of godliness, perhaps with the support and encouragement of one or two fellow-believers, may be adequate to win deliverance from demonic influence. However, in cases involving "inhabitation," possession, or complete dominance of the person by the demon or demons, it may be important to involve others in more sustained prayer support and in the actual casting-out process. An example that underscores this distinction is that there were some demons which the disciples were unable to cast out, although they clearly had been successful in other instances (see Matt. 17:14–21). It appears that more difficult cases require special preparation.

It is important to recognize that deliverance and exorcism are more similar to each other than either is to the approaches we have considered to this point. It is also important to recognize that both should be reserved for difficult cases. These include instances in which the general methods of submission to God and resisting the devil, utilizing the armor of God, and discipline for godliness have been ineffective, yet the afflicted individual sincerely is seeking to be freed from demonic influence to honor God. This is especially relevant when the person is so completely under the control of demonic influence that he or she seems unable to choose.

Even when casting out or exorcism of demons is appropriate, all the practices that have already been described need to precede and follow the actual act. Further, if the casting out has been done without the individual's clear request and consent, we must be aware that he or she may choose to be possessed once more rather than take advantage of the freedom thus granted.

Several elements appear essential in the lives of any who would attempt to deliver others from demon possession. The first is the personal salvation of the individuals involved in the process. Second, there should be a consistent life of personal holiness. Third, there should be a significant degree of personal spiritual maturity. Fourth, there should be confession of all known sin. Fifth, it is wise to make a renewed personal commitment to God, affirming his sovereignty, and submitting to his will. Sixth, it is important to have a good biblical knowledge of the character of Satan and demons. Seventh, it is important to pray for spiritual wisdom, including the gift of discernment of spirits. Finally, it is wise to arrange a support team of other individuals with similar spiritual maturity who are prepared to help in the process of casting out the evil spirits.[14]

It is important to note that there is no magic in such a procedure. What is required is disciplined, obedient submission to God and the active seeking of his will in our lives.

Dickason's comments are helpful at this point. He encourages the use of counseling of all sorts, and reports working cooperatively with a variety of counselors. He notes:

Actually all forms of good counsel may be heeded— medical, psychological, and pastoral. Anything that improves the ability of a person to function psychologically, spiritually, and socially is of help in battle with demonic forces.

Pastoral counseling is most appropriate in spiritual warfare, since this should be the special concern of such counseling. . . . There are several reasons for this. First, the person who suspects he is demonized should have his condition evaluated by a counselor with skill and experience in this area. There must be proper diagnosis as to whether he really is demonized or not. The diagnosis determines the approach taken to getting help. Second, a skilled counselor can help the counselee to clarify and examine symptoms and evidence. He would seek to help him distinguish between his own thoughts and demonic thoughts. Third, the pastoral counselor aids in gaining perspective and gives encouragement regarding the warfare. Finally, he may help the counselee in actual confrontation and dismissal of spirits.

The major purpose in counseling and confrontation is not to expel the demons but to facilitate dependency upon God and personal development of the counselee.[15]

The key issues are the individual's personal relationship to God, and that glory be drawn to God. Also, we must remember to submit ourselves to God, even in the matter of deliverance, affirming as Jesus taught us, "thy will be done" (Matt. 6:10).

Delay in the removal of demons from believers is not uncommon; it may even be a good thing. Jesus and his disciples at times encountered resistance and delay. Dickason reports, "Several counselors have noted that delay is rather normal today, since we are not working miracles to prove the deity of Christ and are not invested with miraculous gifts."[16] Dickason cites Conrad Murrell, Grayson H. Ensign, Edward Howe, and Merrill F. Unger as those who agree with this view. Such has been my experience as well.[17]

Several principles must be considered concerning God's purposes in allowing demons to remain influential in the lives of believers.

First, it is helpful to reflect on the process of occupation of the land of Canaan under the leadership of Joshua. God did not give the entire land to the Israelites at once. Rather they had to fight for possession. The fight itself was beneficial in producing toughness, persistence, faithfulness, and unity among the Israelites. So, too, God expects you and me to be involved in spiritual warfare in an ongoing manner, thus growing tougher and wiser, as well as more dependent upon the body of Christ and the Holy Spirit.

Second, even as occupation of the land progressed, pockets of resistance remained that were yet to be eradicated. So, in the life of the believer, the transformation to godly living is an ongoing process. It should not be surprising that it takes time to eradicate lifelong, sinful habit-patterns and replace them with patterns of godly living. We should recognize that the world, the flesh, and the devil work together in resisting this process of transformation toward godliness. We, too, are involved in a battle.

Third, God suggested to the Israelites that it would not be good for the land to become uninhabited, lest it become overgrown by thorns and invaded by wild animals. This is true for the believer as well. We are warned that it is not enough to cast out demons. It takes time to develop the godly patterns of living that must take the place of evil lest there be even worse demonic influence (see Matthew 12:43–45).

Fourth, God does not work in our lives against our wills. The delivered person must be committed to renouncing the patterns of sin that have given a place for the entry of demonic influence before that person can be fully freed.

There may be other purposes as well, such as the development of spiritual discipline, the strengthening and sensitizing effects of affliction, the need to learn to rely and depend upon God, and/or other specific divine purposes, such as were described in the life of Job.

We also need to understand God's purposes in deliverance. Foremost among these is that God's will be done and that glory and honor be given to his name. This has important implications for us, including many of the factors just discussed.

Successful deliverance will have a number of effects on the person freed from demonic influence. Not all of these effects seem immediately pleasant, though all lead toward honoring God. Among the less pleasant effects are emotional and physical weariness; loss of various occult powers, such as clairvoyance and secret knowledge; the loss of the ability to speak in unknown languages; and reversal of "charmed" healings.

Positive changes include a new sense of freedom of thought

and action; renewed capacity for peace and love, though the initial process of deliverance may involve great turmoil; freedom from voices in the mind which may accuse of wrongdoing, or incite to hatred and violence; freedom from suicidal impulses and depression; freedom from demonically induced ailments; restoration of personal worth and identity; ability to choose; improved social relationships, including marriage; increased trust and respect for Christ; increased awareness of and resistance to evil; and, most importantly, freedom for spiritual growth.

Successful deliverance will be accomplished with greater or lesser speed depending upon such factors as the determination and spiritual maturity of the counselee as well as the experience and wisdom of the counselor.

As was emphasized earlier, our first focus ought always to be on carrying out fully that which is clearly and explicitly taught in Scripture. To fail to do so is to join with King Saul in his rebellion toward God, a rebellion which occasioned God's rejection of him as king. Saul's initial sin was that he did not carry out God's command to "utterly destroy" all in Amalek. God's judgment of Saul, in turn, deserves our attention:

"Has the Lord as much delight in burnt offerings and sacrifices as in obeying the voice of the Lord? Behold, to obey is better than sacrifice, and to heed than the fat of rams. For rebellion is as the sin of divination, and insubordination is as iniquity and idolatry. Because you have rejected the word of the Lord, He has also rejected you from being king." (1 Sam. 15:22–23)

As we have seen, idolatry involves the worship of demons, and ultimately of Satan, their head. With Saul, Satan succeeded by encouraging him that he need not fully obey God, rather than by inviting Saul directly to worship Satan. Notice that the failure to obey God is described as divination (or witchcraft) and idolatry. Perhaps this is an example of the subtle working of the deceiver; rather than enticing us to worship a false god, he encourages us to set ourselves up as gods.

It should come as no great surprise, then, that God chooses not to deliver us from demons while we are actively involved in worship of them! Renunciation of all sin and false worship is vital to any true deliverance. But beyond that, there must be submission to God in a loving and obedient manner.

SUMMARY

Because people function as wholes, there is an interaction among the various aspects. Effective counseling must deal with all the aspects of the person. This means that teamwork is normally the preferred mode of help.

The basic spiritual resources provided for becoming free from demonic influence include the process of submission to God and resisting the devil; equipping oneself with the armor of God (which includes salvation, truth, righteousness, peace, faith, and the Word of God); and becoming a slave to righteousness. These require continuing personal involvement on the part of the individual who desires freedom from demonic influence. As we engage in this process, we progressively gain freedom from habitual sinful patterns and desires, and from Satan's ability to exploit these to control us.

God has provided numerous spiritual resources to aid us in submitting to him and resisting demonic influence. These resources begin with the meaning and purpose in life which God gives to each of his children. There is also the support and help of others, prayer, fellowship, worship, service, and the study, memorization of and meditation in Scripture. Regular use of these resources is clearly and consistently taught in Scripture as the means of gaining freedom from the bondage of sin and Satan.

Although exorcism or the casting out of demons is never explicitly commanded by Scripture, and no specific techniques are offered, it appears that a legitimate role exists for these practices. In those instances in which the individual is so dominated by demons that he or she is unable to choose to engage in the other processes, exorcism or casting out is appropriate. While no specific ritual can be established from Scripture, the basic elements involve commanding the demon or demons to depart from the individual in the name of God. Both before and after this process, all involved should examine themselves to see that they are submitted to God, resisting the devil, and equipping themselves with the armor of God.

In addition to dealing with the spiritual needs of the person, concern must also be addressed to other personal needs, including physical, psychological, social, and occupational functioning. Often, problems in these areas contribute to demonization or result from it. It is to several of these issues that we turn in chapter 11.

CHAPTER ELEVEN

COUNSELING APPROACHES

Chapter 10 dealt with spiritual interventions; this chapter will address other aspects of intervention. Just as demonic influence can affect personality, so physical, emotional, and cognitive functioning may influence a person's susceptibility to demonic influence. For example, a person who suffers from chronic low self-esteem may seek demonic influence in an effort to gain power, influence, or recognition. It is no coincidence that our literature abounds with stories of people who made a pact with the devil.

In the material that follows we will examine spiritual preparations for dealing with demonic influence, methods and goals of counseling, how to assess the various aspects of a counselee's functioning, referral to other helpers, counseling strategies, and the use of spiritual resources.

SPIRITUAL PREPARATIONS

Spiritual preparations have been addressed previously. It is important for the counselor to approach the interventions presented in this chapter with those same spiritual preparations.

1. We must acknowledge that people actually may come under demonic influence or control.

2. We must know the most common historical and behavioral indicators of possible demonic influence.

3. We must be aware that any form of false worship, or any habitual pattern of sinful conduct, makes one potentially liable to demonic influence.

4. It is imperative to ensure the full, voluntary cooperation of the person involved unless he or she is so incapacitated as to be unable to choose to cooperate. To do less is to go beyond what even God would do (also, informed consent is a basic principle of professional ethics).[1] In these ways we may more readily and promptly recognize demonic influence when it is present.

5. The counselor must be spiritually prepared for confronting demonic influence. The Christian counselor—indeed anyone who encounters the demonic—is foolish to proceed without it. Such preparation includes a personal relationship with God; confession and repentance of all known personal sin; and a basic understanding of scriptural principles regarding sin, Satan, and the demonic, as well as the principles and practice of godly living (see chapter 10).

Specifically, as counselors we must submit ourselves to God and be filled with the Holy Spirit, equip ourselves with the resources God provides in the "armor of God," and personally resist Satan in our own lives. This requires practicing the basic spiritual disciplines of confession, prayer, worship, fellowship, Bible study, memorization, meditation, and spiritual service. This is important for the protection of the counselor as well as the person receiving counsel.

METHODS AND GOALS OF COUNSELING

Beyond the preparations for counseling, there are two other major areas of concern in the counseling relationship. The first has to do with the means employed, the second with the goals of counseling. The legitimacy of both means and goals must be evaluated according to biblical teachings.

Methods

We often hear the expression "I'd give anything to. . . ." Such an approach to life is inconsistent with God-given standards, and opens the person to potential demonic influence. In effect, this approach makes the goal, whatever it is, more important than submission to God. It is, therefore, a form of idolatry, and consequently is not the path to freedom from demonic influence.

An example of an unacceptable method is seeking to help an individual overcome homosexual practices through overt heterosexual activities outside of marriage. The goal of overcoming homosexual activity is good, but the means of accomplishing it transgresses biblical standards and thus cannot be condoned.

Another example of unacceptable methods is to encourage counselees to begin to deal with suppressed hostility and rage by imagining they are hitting, kicking, or otherwise harming the individual with whom they are angry. Learning to deal with anger constructively means learning when and how to express it. But to imagine doing so in destructive ways is inconsistent with biblical teachings, particularly when we consider that what we think often leads to corresponding actions (see Proverbs 23:7, Matthew 12:33–37). The goal is good, but the method may make the person vulnerable to demonic influence.

Goals

We are equally concerned with the goals of counseling; they must also be consistent with biblical teachings. One additional concern is that even those goals that seem superficially legitimate may be unacceptable if they are not held in proper priority. Jack's desire to maintain his marriage is a God-honoring goal, but it becomes unacceptable when Jack uses threats, harassment, intimidation, and physical abuse to keep his wife in the relationship. Superficially, it may seem that Jack's problem is the *means* he uses to keep his wife involved with him. However, the *goal* of keeping the marriage together at any cost has become more important to Jack than his submission and obedience to God; in effect, Jack's wife has become his god.

Another example of a problematic goal is seeking to free an individual of guilt regarding sexual promiscuity while that person continues practicing such behavior. Freedom from guilt is a legitimate goal, but not for the individual who continues transgressing God-given standards of conduct. In such instances, guilt is a God-given warning signal that danger lies ahead.

In many instances the methods and goals in question are not so easily evaluated. Thus, a good working knowledge of Scripture is of great value for every counselor, particularly a counselor dealing with the demonically influenced. Since, as we have seen, the number of persons demonically influenced is far greater than most of us have supposed, this is a concern for virtually every counselor.

The significance of recognizing subtle sins cannot be overestimated. Because any habitual sinful pattern provides an avenue for potential demonic influence, we must be concerned especially about those sins that seem to be socially acceptable. Many of these, in devious ways, involve "false gods."

False gods are anything that is more important to a person than his or her relationship and commitment to the living God. These idols may be such diverse things as the car the person drives, the house in which he or she lives, or personal appearance, clothes, athletic success, academic achievement, or business success.

Sadly, most of us—often secretly, or even overtly—admire people who are obsessed with false gods. In this way, we show that we tend to agree with them about the importance of the goals and objects they have chosen. The heart is truly deceitful and desperately wicked; only God can know it fully (Jer. 17:9–10). To be able to recognize some of these more subtle forms of false worship we need to seek God's wisdom diligently and consistently.

People under various degrees of demonic influence, or even those with worldviews different from the Christian worldview, may come to us for help with more limited goals, or quite different goals from what we as Christians might wish. For example, they may not wish to become Christian. Also, they may choose to continue living in a way that we perceive as harmful or sinful.

A couple may be living together without the benefit of marriage. In such instances it is essential to respect the wishes of the person or persons seeking counseling. While it is appropriate to encourage such a couple to consider changing their goals, ultimately the counselor must accept the goal of the counselee, or decline to offer counsel.

ASSESSING THE PROBLEM

One of the most important initial concerns of counseling is the careful assessment of the counselee's current condition. This involves two elements: examining for evidence that demonic influence is present and seeing what other conditions might also be involved. These conditions could account for disturbance in mood, thought or behavior; they may also complicate the primary problem. In any event, they must be identified and dealt with in an appropriate fashion if the person is to become whole. Neglecting to deal with all of them may doom the counselor's efforts to free the person from demonic influence, or may result in a subsequent recurrence of the problem.

For example, depression may result from a number of factors: grief over the loss of a loved one, losing one's job or health, financial reverses, or a variety of other factors; disorders of blood electrolyte levels, perhaps due to illness or the side effects of medication; substance abuse; a brain tumor (benign or cancerous); psychological stresses, such as interpersonal conflict; or chronic fatigue. What could be more discouraging or irresponsible than to provide extended counseling for depression while an untreated medical condition progresses to the danger point?

Similarly, it is both futile and potentially harmful to attempt to expel demons from a person who is suffering from a mental disorder. Given the high degree of similarity in the symptoms of mental disorders and demonic influence noted earlier, considerable care must be given to exploring and evaluating the problem before commencing treatment.

Medical Evaluation

While depression is not generally believed to be an indication of demonic influence, many other conditions which have physical roots may be confused with it. Broadly speaking, these include all of the organic psychotic conditions described previously. Among the physical factors that could account for such disturbances are head injuries, diseases affecting mental functioning (such as a stroke, tumors, Alzheimer's disease, and dementia), the effects of drug toxicity or drug withdrawal (whether legal or illegal), and exposure to environmental toxins.

Referral for appropriate medical evaluation is essential. It is important that the physician be informed that the patient is receiving counseling and also be told of the nature of the problems he or she is experiencing. When demonic influence is suspected it may be especially helpful to refer the person to a Christian physician, or at least to one who is sympathetic with such concerns. In this manner the patient can acknowledge his or her spiritual concerns and receive needed medical evaluation and care without being scorned for personal religious beliefs.

Psychological Evaluation

Besides the fact that their symptoms are similar, physical disorders, mental disorders, and demonic influence may all be present in a counselee since the presence of any one of the three results in greater susceptibility to the others. For this reason, psychological evaluation is needed to discover whether the symptoms may be partly or completely the result of psychological factors. In such an evaluation, the person will be examined for evidence of psychotic conditions in particular, since these may produce symptoms similar to demonic influence. The person will be examined for symptoms of other mental disorders as well. Psychological testing should also be conducted to assess the person's general psychological and intellectual/cognitive functioning.

One dimension of psychological evaluation involves assessing the degree to which the person may be exaggerating or even faking the problem behaviors. Often, a person will pretend to have mental disorders in order to gain various personal or social benefits accorded those presumed to be mentally ill, such as hospitalization or freedom from work and other responsibilities.

Other factors that may be included in psychological evaluation are current intellectual functioning, learning disabilities, neuropsychological functioning, and such aspects of interpersonal behavior as aggressiveness and ability to relate positively with people.

In seeking a psychological evaluation, it is again important to find psychologists who are Christian, or who are at least open-minded about spiritual problems, especially demonic influence. Developing good referral sources is difficult, but essential.

Spiritual Evaluation

Even when physical or psychological disorders have been clearly identified, this does not rule out the possibility of spiritual problems, including demonic influence. Thus, in any instance where demonic influence is a consideration, counselors who are not themselves expert in dealing with spiritual issues, especially those having no experience with demonic influence, will wisely refer the counselee to appropriate spiritual counselors, or involve such individuals in the counseling process. Both Allison and Dickason provide examples of taking this course of action.[2]

Social and Emotional Evaluation

An evaluation of the person's social and emotional circumstances is essential in understanding his or her current functioning. Often this is referred to as a "psychosocial evaluation." Included in such an evaluation, in addition to a history of the current problems, is a description of the person's present living situation, family membership and family history, physical and emotional health, finances, intellectual functioning, employment, and education. Special attention is given to any recent changes in any of these areas.

Personal History

Personal history is generally included in the evaluation of social and emotional circumstances, but additional factors not ordinarily covered in such an evaluation may be essential to discern the presence or absence of demonic influence. Particularly important is historical evaluation for those factors commonly associated with demonic influence, discussed in chapter 8.

Additional elements of personal history to be examined include recent losses of any kind, whether death, divorce, custody changes, moving, being fired or laid off, retirement, broken dreams, disappointment, or financial changes. Even "positive" changes, such as winning the lottery, may have adverse emotional effects.

Other personal-history factors include such things as experiencing physical or sexual abuse, participating in or being exposed to alcohol or drug abuse, parental absence, and social stigmatization. Often, questions like "what is the worst thing that ever happened to you?" and "what is your earliest memory?" prove very helpful in this regard.

Drug and Alcohol Evaluation

A large number of mental disorders may result from or be worsened by the abuse of a variety of substances such as alcohol and prescription or street drugs. Some of the symptoms of substance abuse are similar to those of demonic influence. Thus, it is important to comprehensively evaluate the degree to which use of substances affects the person.

COUNSELING APPROACHES

In general, the approaches to be taken with persons who have come under demonic influence are the same as those for people who do not manifest such difficulties. As we have seen, the entrance of sin into our world has profound implications for the entire created order. First, the whole of Creation, including each person, is tainted with the effects of sin. Second, each person is naturally "bent" toward evil. Third, the earth is the domain of Satan and his demons, thus the potential for people to come under demonic influence is always present. Fourth, we have noted that Satan is a crafty being who chooses those approaches that are most effective in accomplishing his ends. In the contemporary Western world, with its strong materialistic reductionism, it is not surprising that Satan chooses to work within this worldview rather than to appear in an overtly spiritual (immaterial) fashion. Finally, we have seen that physical diseases, mental disorders, and demonic influence are all the result of this process of sin in the world and satanic activity; all are instigated by Satan, yet all serve God's sovereign purposes and are under divine control.

Because of the many fundamental similarities between mental disorders and demonic influence, treatment of these diverse problems often may be approached in similar ways. The commonly accepted approaches to counseling are generally helpful to persons experiencing demonic influence in its more blatant as well as its subtle forms. The one important exception is when demonic influence is so complete that the individual lacks the capacity to choose freedom from demonic control. In these instances, however rare, delivering the person from demonic control is a necessary precursor to counseling. Only then is he or she able to choose continued freedom from demonic control. However, it must be acknowledged that this person may choose to allow, or even to seek, demonic powers and control once more.

One additional precaution is suggested here. Since deliverance and exorcism are essentially religious processes, it is recommended that they be done in a religious setting and by religious counselors, such as pastors and lay Christian ministers. While involuntary treatment for drug and alcohol abuse is permitted by law under certain conditions, the legality of involuntary deliverance or exorcism is likely to be problematic; it is also likely to violate ethical guidelines for professional counselors such as psychiatrists, psychologists, social workers, and marriage and family counselors.

In many respects, involuntary deliverance or exorcism is analogous to involuntarily detoxification for alcohol or drug abuse. Once the involuntary restraints are removed, the person may choose to continue in the treatment and recovery process, or may resume substance use at the first opportunity. Further, even though the person makes the initial choice for continued recovery, he or she may waver and stumble repeatedly before the new patterns of recovery and sobriety become well established. Experience shows that recovered substance abusers undergo an average of three detoxifications before they reach the point of stable abstinence. As more information is gathered on the process of deliverance from demonic influence and possession, similar patterns may emerge. Satan's ways are both devious and truly enslaving. Considerable diligence and persistence, and much help from others, is required to become free from them.

A number of specific counseling strategies are of particular help to those who have come under demonic influence. These include providing emotional support, implementing behavioral change, correcting errors of thought and perception, and confronting patterns of self-deception and denial. It may be helpful to involve the person in both individual and group counseling to facilitate the needed changes.

Providing Emotional Support

"Beginnings are hard; all beginnings are hard," says a character in Chaim Potok's *My Name Is Asher Lev*. Certainly this is true of beginning the radical life-change that is essential to gaining freedom from demonic influence. To successfully undergo this process, the individual must have a great deal of encouragement and emotional support. Counseling is one important way in which emotional support may be provided.

The person undergoing change needs to be encouraged to experience and express his or her emotions. Bitterness, anger, disappointment, discouragement, and other unpleasant emotions (or complex combinations of emotions and thoughts) need to be acknowledged, evaluated, and resolved. Experiences may need to be examined and reinterpreted. Old hurts need to be forgiven and put to rest. Encouragement must be provided to initiate new patterns of interaction with others.

In addition to counseling on an individual basis, the person also needs to deal with emotional issues and to receive support in a group setting such as group counseling may afford. In some instances, this may be accomplished through active involvement in a small "shepherding" or fellowship group in a local church. In such groups, while Bible study is an important part, the focus must be broader, involving fellowship, prayer, mutual support and encouragement, burden-bearing, shared meals, working together on tasks of spiritual service, and corporate prayer.

Jane Jane came complaining of such profound depression that she needed antidepressant medication as well as counseling. When I first saw her she had been involved for some time in an extramarital affair. A Christian, she knew that the affair was wrong; she was experiencing considerable guilt, yet she found her marriage so unsatisfying that she was reluctant to give up the other man.

Initially, counseling provided most of Jane's much-needed emotional support. With my encouragement, she gradually became more involved in a few friendships which provided acceptance, support, and belonging.

As Jane and I worked together we discovered that she had a lot of resentment toward her husband. Some of it grew out of misunderstandings and misinterpretations of his interactions with her; these needed correction. Other hurts needed to be forgiven. As we worked through these issues, we also gave attention to a more realistic appraisal of her relationship with the other man. Gradually, Jane decided to break off her affair, though three or four times she reinitiated contact. As her depression and guilt lifted, and as she began to understand and accept herself as a person whom God had made and whom God loved just as she was, Jane gradually developed the desire to deal with problems in her relationship with her husband. At this point our emphasis shifted toward developing new patterns of behavior which would be more productive in dealing with him (see below).

Correcting Thought and Perception

Most of us carry with us some degree of distortion in our thoughts and perceptions. Though many are able to live productively despite such distortions, distortions in thought are disabling in some instances. The modern approach of cognitive behavior therapy specializes in correcting patterns of thinking and perception that contribute to guilt, depression, anxiety, and a variety of other mental problems. We find in Scripture that one of the basic remedies for errors in thinking is through learning and meditating on God's Word. Psalm 119 addresses this matter at length; see also Jeremiah 17:10 and Romans 1:21–2:2.

Sometimes, thinking disorders result from conscious or unconscious efforts at self-deception. Most of the classic defense mechanisms described in the psychological literature are forms of distorted thinking and perception. At times, misperceptions and thinking errors are the unwitting result of exposure to the sinful patterns of others. For example, the person who grows up with alcoholic parents is commonly exposed to certain patterns of behavior which result in distorted thinking and behavior patterns that often produce mental disorders, adult alcoholism, and perhaps demonic influence.[3]

Jane's father was extremely critical. When she failed to measure up to his expectations, no reason or explanation was considered valid. His wrath and punishment were certain, but forgiveness seemed impossible. As we worked together, Jane discovered that she was unable to believe that others, even God, could forgive her. She in turn found it difficult to forgive those who offended her. Gradually she was able to discover that others did forgive her, and she began to experience God's forgiveness. She also was able to begin to forgive those who had offended her. Through this process Jane gradually changed her belief about being unforgivable.

Behavioral Change

As a general rule, one dimension of being under demonic influence is the presence of various sinful or destructive patterns of behavior. Typically, behaviors involve a complex pattern, an interplay among thoughts, feelings, and behavior. For instance, at Satan's urging, Eve chose to eat the forbidden fruit. She doubted God's word that she would surely die (thought), she desired to know as God knew (emotion/motivation), and she took the fruit and ate it (behavior).

Behavior patterns that lead up to demonic influence are complex. Typically, they involve both the presence of sinful behavior and the absence of alternative godly conduct. The problem with a thief is not only that he or she takes things that belong to others. It also includes elements of greed, ingratitude, and selfishness—thoughts and feelings—and the absence of desirable behaviors such as working to meet personal needs and giving to meet the needs of others (see Ephesians

4:17–24). Behavioral psychologists such as B. F. Skinner have shown that problem behavior involves both behavioral excesses and deficiencies. For example, the person who throws tantrums or is aggressive also lacks appropriate negotiating and cooperative behaviors.[4]

In Jane's case, the fact that she was seeing another man was an obvious behavior problem. As I came to know her better, I learned that part of what was missing was the effective communication of anger toward her husband, followed by an effective solving of problems in their relationship. As we worked together, she learned how to communicate disappointments and hurts to her husband as well as how to invite and encourage him to share such experiences with her. Often this process is referred to as assertiveness training.[5] For Jane, the goal was to develop intimacy with her husband through the sharing of thoughts and feelings, thus paving the way for realistic problem solving.

Confronting Self-Deception and Denial

Jeremiah tells us that "the heart is deceitful above all things and desperately wicked . . . ." Many other Scriptures echo this theme. Furthermore, the devil is the father of lies. Thus, it should come as no surprise that people with mental disorders and especially those with problems of demonic influence engage in self-deception and denial. In most instances, the denial and distortion in which they engage is subtle; it is rare that we fall for blatant untruths; but tainted or twisted truth may deceive us fairly readily.

The basic antidote to deception is truth. There is often no better way to deal with such patterns than to begin with the truth of Scripture. There are many ways to do this, both for Christians and for unbelievers. Persons concerned with demonic influence are generally professing believers; thus, there is an implicit commitment to an acceptance of Scripture. At the same time, the counselee may also be openly or subtly rebellious against Scripture, and this attitude must be addressed.

Jane recognized from the outset that her involvement with the "other man" was wrong. She vacillated between being committed to him and recognizing that he was exploitive and dishonest with her at times. One task was to help her see both the good and the bad at the same time, thus making it more difficult for her to vacillate in this relationship. Eventually, this process helped her with the decision to end the relationship.

A second dimension of dealing with Jane's problems was to help her view her relationship with her husband accurately. She tended to blame him for all that was wrong and to discount her role in their problems. As we explored their relationship, however, several problems emerged. The first was unforgiveness for offenses he had made over the years. We worked together on learning to forgive and put away past offenses.

Jane also discovered a vengeful attitude toward her husband whenever he disappointed her. She confessed that she used to kick him while he was asleep. Another time, she discovered that she got back at him for not spending time with her by scheduling appointments which she knew he would not want to keep. She also recognized that he was quite tired and tended to be more irritable under such circumstances. As we explored this together, she was able to allow him free time for rest and recreation, even if it meant watching the TV.

A second dimension of dealing with this pattern was for her to learn to ask her husband more directly for what she wanted him to do, and to express appreciation for his cooperation. Initially, she tended to become angry with him if he in any way communicated that he was not glad to do as she requested.

A third dimension of dealing with this problem was Jane's discovery that she did not trust other people, and doubted they would like her; hence, she did not try to develop friendships with other women. Part of this grew out of her relationship with her mother.

Group Counseling

Although much of what we have discussed is best accomplished in individual counseling, some things are most effectively addressed in a group. Two of these are social-relationship issues, and issues involving self-deception and denial. Groups can also have a powerful effect in correcting errors in perception and thinking.

The literature on alcohol and substance abuse focuses on pervasive lying as a common part of the life patterns of abusers. It is so common that the following joke is considered a truism: "How do you know an alcoholic is lying? His lips are moving." It is less clearly documented, but it seems likely that those involved in overt demonic influence may also practice subtle patterns of dishonesty, especially with themselves. Thus, group counseling is an important method of treatment for such problems.

Although Jane did not choose to receive group counseling, it is often helpful for those with similar problems. A large part of Jane's difficulty was relational; groups provide a helpful setting for learning new ways of relating.

A major factor that may lead people into demonic influence is the desire for personal significance. This often grows out of an experience of being a social misfit. Further, extensive involvement in demonic influence requires personal passivity, and may in other ways interfere with normal social relationships. Thus, deficiencies in social relationships are likely to be common. For all of these reasons, group counseling is an advisable part of the counseling process.

USE OF SPIRITUAL RESOURCES

As already suggested, the person seeking freedom from demonic influence needs both counseling and spiritual development. He or she ought to be involved in active worship, personal Bible study, fellowship with other believers, and active personal service (ministry) of some sort, and should maintain a consistent prayer life. Being personally discipled or an active participant in a small fellowship or study group is particularly important. This fosters spiritual growth, and also contributes to social and emotional development.

While a balance of work, worship, rest, and recreation must be achieved, it is important that the individual not have large periods of free time available, especially initially. The saying, "idle hands are the devil's workshop," is most true of people who are seeking to break free from old sinful patterns involving demonic influence. Being involved in meaningful activities is one of the most powerful antidotes to coming once more under satanic influence. The biblical pattern is "put off sinful ways . . . and put on righteousness" (Eph. 4:13–31, 5:11–18).[6] The value of this approach is underscored by the biblical alternatives: we are either slaves to sin or servants to righteousness.

SUMMARY

In counseling with those under demonic influence, several factors are important.

First, the counselor must be prepared spiritually, especially if the spiritual dimensions of the problems are to be met. Second, it is important that the goals of counseling, and the methods of achieving them, be scrutinized to ensure they are consistent with biblical principles.

Third, all the dimensions of the problems need to be evaluated—spiritual, medical, psychological, social-emotional, personal history, and drug and alcohol abuse. Each problem area discovered needs to be addressed in treatment; many aspects of this process will require cooperation with or referral to others. The ideal arrangement is for all individuals involved to work together in an effective team. Fourth, counseling in both individual and group modes may be required. Such counseling should address a number of dimensions, including the provision of emotional support, correcting distortions in thinking and perception, fostering behavioral changes, and dealing with self-deception and denial.

Finally, spiritual resources need to be utilized to support and aid the major changes the individual must undergo to effectively gain freedom from demonic influence. It is important to remember that freedom is not gained by the mere absence of evil spirits; it comes only when the person is effectively brought under the power of God through personal commitment and the support and encouragement of others.

CHAPTER TWELVE

SUMMARY AND CONCLUSIONS

Despite the materialistic bent of our culture, interest in the demonic is growing. Demon possession is only one of a variety of ways in which Satan and his emissaries work. Consequently, Christians must learn to deal with demonic influence in all of its many guises regardless of whether we believe that Christians can actually be possessed.

An implacable foe of God, Satan seeks to attack and destroy all who serve God. Satan is a living, active, powerful, personal being. Formerly an angel of God, Satan sought to usurp God's throne. As a consequence, he was thrown out of heaven, and his activities now center around the earth. His methods are varied. Though he is the personification of evil, he may appear as an angel of light. His methods include temptation, deception, slander, fostering guilt, encouraging violence and greed, and a host of other devices. He chooses those approaches which most effectively serve his ends, and he uses different techniques in different cultures and in different historical periods.

Satan's end is sure. He was defeated by the death and resurrection of Christ. Meanwhile, however, he remains a powerful and dangerous foe who must be resisted, using the resources which God provides. The believer is assured that nothing can separate him or her from the love of God, and that Satan's powers are limited and governed by God's sovereign hand. Yet, we must be ever mindful that we are in the midst of a desperate spiritual war, and be constantly on guard.

Satan is not alone in his rebellion against God and in his enmity toward all who would serve God. In his rebellion he took with him a host of angelic beings, now demons, who sided with him and now exercise his bidding. Demons extend his influence over the entire earth.

A key element of Satan's plan is to foster spiritual blindness and encourage all manner of false worship, particularly idolatry. Worshiping any thing other than the true God in the true way is idolatry. All idolatry, in essence, involves the worship of demons and, therefore, of Satan himself. Thus Satan's plot to usurp God's place continues.

There is disagreement about whether Christians can be demon possessed; most evangelicals believe that the indwelling presence of the Holy Spirit prevents possession of believers. Regardless of the position one takes on this matter, it is hard to avoid the conclusion that believers may be attacked, enticed, accused, presented with false teaching, and otherwise influenced by Satan and demons. Such was true in the lives of the apostles, and it is doubtless true in ours as well.

MARKS OF THE DEMON POSSESSED

A number of accounts of demon possession are presented in the Bible, chiefly in the Gospels. From these we find that those who are so possessed show a number of striking features. Among these are acts of magic, supernatural strength and knowledge, physical maladies—such as deafness, blindness, and epileptic-like seizures—altered voices, the absence of social graces, self-harming activities, fierce and violent behavior, and the appearance of distinct personalities. Unfortunately, these patterns are also observed in those who are mentally disordered.

Demonic influence varies widely, from the merest suggestion or enticement to inhabitation and almost total domination of the individual. Symptoms also vary, from the forms found in the Gospel accounts to the magical and oracular powers of the magicians and sorcerers of Egypt, and the astrologers and Chaldeans of Babylon. Contemporary parallels include witch doctors in Third World cultures, and what Scott Peck calls the "truly evil people" of our own culture.

Satan and his demons also produce physical disease and natural disaster; they foster spiritual doubt, and perverted forms of worship. His deceptiveness is so effective that often we are oblivious of Satan's activities. Such deception, of course, is a key element of his strategy and grows from his nature as a liar.

He and his demons encourage the separation of the spiritual and the material, the sacred and the secular. As a result of this deception, we ignore one important aspect or another of God's world and of our own nature as bearers of his image. This error takes two forms: materialism, which perceives that what exists is physical or material in essence, and spiritualistic reductionism, which denies the reality or significance of the physical or material realm. In our society, unbelievers tend to hold to the former while many Christians, perhaps in reaction to that, adhere to the latter. Both are distortions; Satan can use either half-truth to distract us from the whole truth and thus subtly distract us from accurately perceiving ourselves and God's Creation.

Spiritualistic reductionism views God as active in the spiritual realm, but discounts his involvement in ordinary events of the created order. For example, God is seen as active in "miraculous" healings, but not in surgery or the use of medication, or in the other, slower processes that are often attributed to "Mother Nature."

In reality, all of Creation is sustained moment by moment by God's power. Thus, all that happens, even the feeding of a single sparrow or the falling of a hair, is a result of God's action.

God is active in both the material and spiritual aspects of our lives; so too is Satan. Although Satan and his demons are spiritual beings, their influence extends over both material and spiritual aspects of our lives and world. As a result, in countering the demonic we need to be mindful of all these aspects.

One of Satan's ploys is to use methods that simulate familiar events that we normally tolerate. In this way, Satan is largely able to escape detection within any given culture. Missionaries and foreign nationals report that they are much more able to spot evidence of satanic activity in unfamiliar cultures than in their own. Such factors as widespread materialistic naturalism, and possibly the strong, historic, Christian influence in the United States, may account for the relatively infrequent occurrence of demonic possession seen in the United States. But the recent decline of Christian influence seems to parallel a rise in overt evil activities.

Satan's efforts to influence are continuous and pervasive. Scripture warns repeatedly that Christians will be the targets of these efforts, and that precautions must be taken. While non-Christians are also subject to the influence of Satan, their relationship to him is very different. They belong to his kingdom, hence they are his agents along with the demons. He may use and exploit them, often without their awareness, but he is not at enmity with them.

THE TWO KINGDOMS

There are but two spiritual kingdoms: the kingdom of God, and that of the prince of the power of the air, Satan himself. All false worship involves choosing to side with Satan. In fact, all are born into Satan's kingdom; the individual must make a personal choice to enter into the kingdom of heaven. Is it surprising that Satan views people who make this choice as deserters?

As a part of his efforts to thwart God's plan and usurp God's throne, Satan attacks all who serve God. This activity began with his approach to Eve in the form of a serpent in the Garden of Eden and it included his destruction of Job's property, family, and health. During Christ's life on earth, Satan tried several times to get him to forsake the plan established before the foundation of the earth. Satan attacked the apostles. Clearly all believers are targets of Satan's efforts, either through direct attack or through crafty attempts to influence them in whatever ways best suit his objectives.

The first sin of Adam and Eve had dramatic and far-reaching effects on the entire Creation. Separation from God and personal sinfulness became the lot of all persons. The whole of Creation was harmed, with the result that predation, sickness, death, and natural disaster became commonplace. The occurrence of mental disorders is one aspect of this change. To fully understand the relationship between mental disorders and demonic influence it is necessary to understand the interrelationships among personal sinfulness, the sin of others, and the many effects of sin on our world.

MENTAL DISORDERS AND THE DEMONIC

Mental disorders, as currently conceived by the American Psychiatric Association's *Diagnostic and Statistical Manual of Mental Disorders,* include a wide range of symptom patterns which stem from a variety of causes, including genetics, illness, injury, trauma, biochemical imbalances in brain functioning, and psychological and behavioral disturbances. Even some behaviors considered criminal are included in the diagnostic system as mental disorders.

Evidence is growing that biological factors play a role in many mental disorders, either as a direct cause or as a contributing factor. Manic depressive disorders and Alzheimer's disease are examples.

Virtually all the symptoms of demon possession found in biblical accounts overlap with those included in mental disorders. Thus the two conditions cannot be distinguished on the basis of symptoms alone.

However, given the strong role of biological factors in mental disorders, especially those which resemble demon possession, it seems unlikely that mental disorders and demon possession are merely different labels for the same problem. In contemporary American culture it is likely that demonic influence will be most common in persons who do not show symptoms of mental disorders; these are the people whom Scott Peck terms "truly evil." Often, mental disorders are found in those who must deal with the truly evil ones on a daily basis, such as family members.

Because difficulties in one aspect of personal functioning make the individual more vulnerable to problems in other areas, it is possible that an individual may be afflicted with both mental disorders and demonic influence or possession at the same time.

Two approaches are helpful in discerning the presence of demonic influence or possession: spiritual discernment and an examination of the person's history for events that predict the likelihood of demonic influence. While neither approach is failsafe, together they can assist in the difficult task of identifying a counselee's problem.

Since a counselee may have more than one type of difficulty, it is strongly recommended that a comprehensive evaluation be done to discover the full range of physical, mental, and spiritual difficulties that may be present.

Exorcism

The Bible does not provide specific instructions on methods of exorcism. At the same time, though it is not clear that what we now call exorcism corresponds to what occurred in the New Testament accounts, exorcism is not prohibited. Thus, this approach may be appropriate at times, though much caution is urged. It seems most appropriate for use when the persons are totally dominated by one or more demons, and therefore seem unable to avail themselves of help when it is offered.

By contrast, much in Scripture speaks of the need to put off sinful ways and replace them with godly ways, to be filled with the Holy Spirit, and to prepare for and be active in a spiritual conflict. We are told to submit to God, to resist the devil, and he will flee. We are told to take up the full armor of God. We are exhorted to forsake the works of darkness, and to put off the "old man" with its lusts. We are told to pray for deliverance from the evil one; Jesus illustrated this in his model prayer for the disciples. These are the spiritual tools and the means that God has provided. As clear biblical commandments, these approaches are always appropriate. If we commit ourselves to them, freedom from demonic influence will come about, gradually and surely, if not dramatically.

Personal, willful involvement is essential to freedom from demonic influence. Thus, it is wise to always involve the individual in the process of seeking deliverance from demonic influence. All of the tools of Christian discipleship, worship, fellowship, and service should be employed, along with the additional benefits which counseling, psychotherapy, and medication can often provide. Only as these are utilized can the person be assured of continued freedom from demonic influence.

Beneficial Counseling Approaches

Counseling approaches that can be of benefit include helping the person recognize and deal constructively with emotions, aiding the person in developing right thinking, changing behavior to bring it into conformity with biblical guidelines, and encouraging healthy relationships.

The local church is an ideal place in which much of the transformation can occur for a person who has been formerly under demonic influence or who has been possessed. This is especially true in small fellowship groups centered on Bible study, worship, prayer, service, and developing personal relationships.

When God met Moses in the desert near Mount Sinai he asked Moses what he had in his hand. When Moses answered that he had a rod, God told him to use it to carry out God's appointed task. When God comes to you and me, I believe he asks the same question. We have seen some of the resources with which God has provided us. Will we use them with gratitude and faithfulness? I pray God that we will!

NOTES

Introduction

1. About a year ago I encountered a book with this title; the author suggests that idolatry is the root of pathology. Although I doubt that the author had in mind a literal understanding of this expression, for me counseling regularly involves taking on the gods. See Merle R. Jordan, *Taking on the Gods: The Task of the Pastoral Counselor* (Nashville: Abingdon, 1986).

2. American Psychiatric Association, *Diagnostic and Statistical Manual of Mental Disorders,* Third Edition, Revised (Washington, D.C.: American Psychiatric Association, 1987).

Chapter 1 The Devil Made Me Do It

1. *Evangelical Press News Service,* May 2, 1986, 9–10.

2. *The Oregonian,* April 10, 1986, A9.

3. *Evangelical Press News Service,* May 2, 1986, 12.

4. "Consulting with Spirits Gains Popularity," *The Oregonian,* May 17, 1987, A24.

5. "Changing Channels," *The Oregonian,* December 19, 1987, C1.

6. Ibid., C3.

7. C. S. Lewis, *Out of the Silent Planet* (New York: Macmillan, 1968; orig. 1938); *Perelandra* (New York: Macmillan, 1968; orig.

1944); *That Hideous Strength* (New York: Macmillan, 1968; orig. 1946).

8. Norman L. Thiessen, *The New Testament Concept of Demonic Possession*, Talbot Theological Seminary, master's thesis, 1975, 2.

9. "Sex Scandals: Graham Blames the Devil." *The Seattle Times*, June 19, 1987.

Chapter 2 Satan Is Alive and Active

1. Michael Green, *I Believe in Satan's Downfall* (Grand Rapids: Eerdmans, 1981).

2. Ibid., 33–42.

3. C. Fred Dickason, *Angels, Elect and Evil* (Chicago: Moody, 1975), 118–19.

4. Green, op. cit., 30.

5. For a general discussion of the names and character of Satan, see ibid., chaps. 11–15; Dickason, op. cit.; Mark I. Bubeck, *The Adversary* (Chicago: Moody, 1975); Herbert Lockyer, *Satan: His Person and Power* (Waco, Tex.: Word, 1980); *Zondervan Pictorial Encyclopedia of the Bible* (Grand Rapids: Zondervan, 1974), 4:282–86; also see Job 1, 2; Zech. 3:1, 2.

6. Rev. 12:9; 20:2.

7. *Zondervan Pictorial Encyclopedia*, 282.

8. Dickason, op. cit., 122; Green, op. cit., 35–42.

9. *Zondervan Pictorial Encyclopedia*, 283.

10. Green, op. cit., 51–52.

11. *Zondervan Pictorial Encyclopedia*, 284; cf. Job 1:7–11; 2:1–6.

12. Ibid., 286.

13. Ibid., 98.

14. For an illustration of this, see Sheldon Vanauken, *A Severe Mercy* (New York: Harper and Row, 1977, 1980). In this biography, Vanauken describes a pact between himself and his wife that nothing would interfere with their relationship. He goes on to tell how they found God and the struggle they experienced in putting him first.

15. Lev. 20:1–5. For a discussion of Molech and other false gods, see "Gods, False," in Charles F. Pfeiffer, Howard F. Vos, and John Rea, eds., *Wycliffe Bible Encyclopedia*, (Chicago: Moody, 1975) 1:697–707.

Chapter 3 Biblical Accounts of Satanic Activity

1. W. Oesterly, *Demon, Demonical Possession, Demoniacs* [1906], cited in Norman L. Thiessen, *The New Testament Concept of Demonic Possession*, Talbot Theological Seminary, 1975, 3–4.

2. Merrill F. Unger, *Biblical Demonology,* (Wheaton, Ill.: Scripture Press, 1952), 90.

3. *Daimonizomai, daimonizomenos, daimonistheis, echon daimonia.* For a discussion of the concept of demon possession, see C. Fred Dickason, *Demon Possession and the Christian* (Chicago: Moody, 1987), especially chap. 3. Other sources include: C. Fred Dickason, *Angels, Elect and Evil* (Chicago: Moody, 1975); Michael Green, *I Believe in Satan's Downfall,* (Grand Rapids: Eerdmans, 1981); Unger, op. cit.

4. See Dickason, op. cit., especially chaps. 1–2.

5. *Zondervan Pictorial Encyclopedia of the Bible,* 2:95.

6. Ibid., 98.

7. E.g., see Dickason, *Angels,* 138.

8. Thiessen, op. cit., chap. 3; Dickason, *Demon Possession,* op. cit., chap. 2.

9. Thiessen, op. cit., 24–28.

10. E.g., Peter; Matt. 16:21–23; Mark 8:31–33; Luke 22:31; Christ's high-priestly prayer, John 17:15; the apostle Paul, 2 Cor. 12:7.

11. For an interesting recent discussion of Satan's character, see William D. Eisenhower, "Your Devil Is Too Small," *Christianity Today,* 1988, 32, no. 10 (July 15), 24–26.

Chapter 4 Faulty Thinking: Separating the Spiritual and the Physical

1. For an interesting discussion of several of these issues see Marguerite Shuster, *Power, Pathology and Paradox* (Grand Rapids: Zondervan, 1987), 55–64; also see Philip Yancey, *"Hearing the World in a Higher Key," Christianity Today* 32, no. 15 (Oct. 21), 24–28.

2. Frederick Copleston, *A History of Philosophy: Volume I, Part 1, Greece and Rome* (Garden City, N.Y.: Image Books, 1962).

3. When God made man he created him out of the dust of the ground, a material substance; then God breathed into him the breath of life so that man became a living being (Gen. 2:7). In addition, God made man in his image, hence spiritual, since God is spirit (Gen. 1:26–27; cp. John 4:23–24). Thus, to deal faithfully with the biblical evidence we must recognize that man is both material and immaterial. For a discussion, see David G. Myers and Malcolm Jeeves, *Psychology Through the Eyes of Faith* (New York: Harper and Row, 1987) chapter 5.

In contrast, John Cooper speaks in favor of dualism and against unity in "Dualism and the Biblical View of Human Beings" (1), *Reformed Journal*, September, 1982, pp. 13–16 and "Dualism and the Biblical View of Human Beings" (2), *Reformed Journal*, October 1982, pp. 16–18; also see Ranald Macaulay and Jerram Barrs, *Being Human: The Nature of Spiritual Experience* (Downers Grove, Ill.: InterVarsity, 1978); Malcolm A. Jeeves, *Psychology and Christianity: The View Both Ways* (Downers Grove, Ill.: InterVarsity, 1976); Richard Bube, *The Human Quest* (Waco, Tex.: Word, 1971).

4. For related discussion see Myers and Jeeves, op. cit., chapter 2; Richard Bube, op. cit.

5. R. J. Ritzema, "Attribution to supernatural causation: an important component of religious commitment?" *Journal of Psychology and Theology*, 1979, 7, pp. 286–93; Kenneth I. Pergament and J. Hahn, *God and the Just World: Causal and Coping Attributions to God in Health Situations*, paper presented at the Annual Meeting of the American Psychological Association, Toronto, August, 1984.

6. James Houston, *I Believe in the Creator* (Grand Rapids: Eerdmans, 1980).

7. See Mark 10:6; Rom. 1:20; 8:22; 2 Pet. 3:4; Rev. 3:14.

8. For a discussion of this conflict, see C. Fred Dickason, *Angels, Elect and Evil* (Chicago, Moody, 1975), and Dickason, *Demon Possession and the Christian* (Chicago, Moody, 1987).

9. Charles C. Ryrie, *The Ryrie Study Bible* (Chicago: Moody, 1976, 1978), 1520.

10. Jay Adams, *Competent to Counsel* (Grand Rapids: Zondervan, 1970).

11. Walter A. Elwell, ed., *Evangelical Dictionary of Theology* (Grand Rapids: Baker, 1984), 299–300.

12. See Henry C. Thiessen, *Lectures in Systematic Theology* (Grand Rapids: Eerdmans, 1979).

13. This belief, though widespread, is considered by evangelical scholars to be false. For the believer, eternal life is a gift granted by God (see, e.g., Rom. 3:23). Apart from God, the judgment of death has already been passed on all men (John 3:16–19).

Chapter 5 Mental Illness

1. Thomas S. Szasz, *The Myth of Mental Illness* (New York: Harper and Row, 1961).

2. For a brief discussion see Rodger K. Bufford, "Mental Illness,

Models of," in David G. Benner, ed., *Baker Encyclopedia of Psychology* (Grand Rapids: Baker, 1985). For a more extended discussion, see James C. Coleman, James N. Butcher, and Robert C. Carson, *Abnormal Psychology and Modern Life*, 8th ed. (Glenview, Ill.: Scott, Foresman and Company, 1987), especially chapters 3–4.

3. American Psychiatric Association, *Diagnostic and Statistical Manual of Mental Disorders*, Third Edition, Revised (DSM-III-R) (Washington, D.C.: American Psychiatric Association, 1987).

4. Leonard T. Ullmann, and Leonard Krasner, *A Psychological Approach to Abnormal Behavior* (Englewood Cliffs, N.J.: Prentice-Hall, 1969), especially see chapters 8–9; Coleman, Butcher, and Carson, op. cit., chapter 2; Harold I. Kaplan and Benjamin J. Sadock, eds., *Comprehensive Textbook of Psychiatry/IV* (Baltimore: Williams and Wilkins, 1985).

5. P. H. Blaney, "Implications of the medical model and its alternatives," *American Journal of Psychiatry*, 1975, *132*, pp. 911–14. The second definition is probably closest to the view underlying the diagnostic manual. Further, the more analogical definitions (3 and 4) closely resemble the alternative models in some respects. See American Psychiatric Association, DSM-III-R, op. cit.

6. American Psychiatric Association, *Diagnostic and Statistical Manual: Mental Disorders* (DSM-I) (Washington, D.C.: American Psychiatric Association, 1952). See also second edition, 1968.

7. *Diagnostic and Statistical Manual of Mental Disorders*, Third Edition, Revised 1980. Also see DSM-III-R, footnote 3.

8. Henry Weinstein, M.D., "Workshop on Irritable Bowel Syndrome," Portland Adventist Medical Center, Feb. 5, 1987.

9. Michael J. Goldstein, Bruce L. Baker, and Kay R. Jamison, *Abnormal Psychology*, 2d ed. (Boston: Little, Brown, 1986), 233–42.

10. See Ullmann and Krasner, op. cit., 125–30.

11. See Bufford, op. cit. For more detail, see Ullmann and Krasner, op. cit., chap. 12. For a more recent statement of a similar view, see Albert Bandura, *Social Foundations of Thought and Action* (Englewood Cliffs, N.J.: Prentice-Hall, 1986).

12. A. S. Gurman and D. P. Kniskern, eds., *Handbook of Family Therapy* (New York: Bruner/Mazel, 1981).

13. John C. Carter and Bruce Narramore, *The Integration of Psychology and Theology* (Grand Rapids: Zondervan, 1979).

14. For a brief summary of Christian perspectives, see D. G. Benner, "Christian Counseling and Psychotherapy," in Benner, ed., op. cit., 158–64. Some examples of Christian approaches to counseling include: Jay Adams, *Competent to Counsel* (Grand Rapids: Baker,

1970); William Backus and Marie Chapian, *Telling Yourself the Truth* (Minneapolis: Bethany Fellowship, 1980); Gary R. Collins, *Helping People Grow* (Santa Ana, Calif.: Vision House, 1980); Mark P. Cosgrove and James D. Mallory, Jr., *Mental Health: A Christian Approach* (Grand Rapids: Zondervan, 1977); Lawrence J. Crabb, Jr., *Basic Principles of Biblical Counseling* (Grand Rapids: Zondervan, 1975); William T. Kirwan, *Biblical Concept for Christian Counseling* (Grand Rapids: Baker, 1984).

15. E.g., see Adams, op. cit.; Backus and Chapian, op. cit.; Crabb, op. cit.

16. J. Harold Ellens, "Counseling and Psychotherapy: Theological Themes," in Benner, op. cit., 249.

17. Carter and Narramore, op. cit.; Cosgrove and Mallory, op. cit.

18. Dave Hunt and T. A. McMahon, *The Seduction of Christianity* (Eugene, Ore.: Harvest House, 1986), 190–91.

19. Jay E. Adams, op. cit.; Martin and Deidre Bobgan, *The Psychological Way: The Spiritual Way* (Minneapolis: Bethany Fellowship, 1979); William Kirk Kilpatrick, *Psychological Seduction* (Nashville: Nelson, 1983).

20. J. Robertson McQuilkin, "The Behavioral Sciences Under the Authority of Scripture," cited in Lawrence J. Crabb, Jr., *Effective Biblical Counseling* (Grand Rapids: Zondervan, 1978).

21. Adams, op. cit., 29.

22. Adams, op. cit.; Crabb, op. cit.; Kirwan, op. cit.

23. For an example of a responsible handling of these issues presented in a brief, readable form, see Cosgrove and Mallory, op. cit.; I recommend this book highly.

Chapter 6 Mental Disorders

1. American Psychiatric Association, *Diagnostic and Statistical Manual of Mental Disorders*, Third Edition, Revised (DSM-III-R) (Washington, D.C.: 1987). This manual was developed with an explicit goal of making it conform as closely as possible with the *International Classification of Diseases*, Ninth Edition–Clinical Modification (ICD-9-CM), thus it is also largely consistent with the international classification system for mental disorders.

2. *Diagnostic and Statistical Manual*, 3d ed., 23.

3. Ibid., 24.

4. Harold I. Kaplan and Benjamin J. Sadock, *Comprehensive*

Textbook of Psychiatry/IV (Baltimore: Williams and Wilkins, 1985) 1754–60.

5. Surgeon General's Report on AIDS (Washington, D.C.: U.S. Government Printing Office, 1987).

6. Ibid.

7. DSM-III-R, 20.

8. Ibid., 30.

9. Ibid., 53.

10. Ibid., 98.

11. Surgeon General's Report, op. cit.

12. "Psychological and Social Considerations in Helping People Cope with Aids." *Behavior Today* (New York: Atcom Publishing, 1987), 3.

13. DSM-III-R, 255.

14. Ibid., 271–72.

15. Corbett Thigpen and Harvey M. Cleckley, *The Three Faces of Eve* (New York: Popular Library, 1957); Flora Rheta Schreiber, *Sybil* (New York: Warner Books, 1973).

16. S. I. McMillen, *None of These Diseases* (revised) (Old Tappan, N.J.: Revell, 1983).

17. T. B. Baker, "Models of Addiction," *Journal of Abnormal Psychology*, 1988, pp. 97.

18. Kaplan and Sadock, op. cit., 1023–24.

19. Jay E. Adams, *Competent to Counsel* (Grand Rapids: Baker, 1970); e.g., see p. 48.

20. Kaplan and Sadock, op. cit., 1126–28; 1130–31.

21. Craig W. Ellison, "Spiritual Well-Being: Conceptualization and Measurement," *Journal of Psychology and Theology*, 1983, *11*, pp. 330–40.

22. David B. Hawkins, *Interpersonal Behavior Traits, Spiritual Well-being and Their Relationships to Blood Pressure* (Portland Ore.: Theological Research Exchange Network, 1986); Rodger K. Bufford, *The Relationship Between Spiritual Well-Being and Physical Health*, paper presented at the Christian Association for Psychological Studies Western Regional Meeting, Seattle, June 1987.

23. *Diagnostic and Statistical Manual* 2d ed., 44. In DSM-III, Ego-Dystonic Homosexuality was included as a specific disorder, but only for persons who experience unwanted arousal to members of the same sex and desire to develop or increase heterosexual arousal. DSM-III reports: "This category is reserved for homosexuals for whom changing sexual orientations is a persistent concern" (p. 382). In DSM-III-R there is no specific reference to Ego-Dystonic Homosexuality except in

the index, which refers the reader to the residual category, *Sexual Dysfunctions Not Otherwise Specified*. However, there is no hint in the text that Ego-Dystonic Homosexuality should be classified here. This is consistent with the growing view among mental-health professionals that homosexuality, as such, is normal and thus should not be considered the focus of treatment.

24. Ibid., 44.

25. The Bible teaches that death is a blessing from God (Gen. 3:22–24), and that even human suffering produces good (Rom. 8:28).

26. John Money, "Sin, Sickness, or Status? Homosexual Gender Identity and Psychoneuroendocrinology," *American Psychologist* 42, no. 4 (April) 1987, 384–99.

27. Leonard Ullmann and Leonard Krasner, *A Psychological Approach to Abnormal Behavior* (Englewood Cliffs, N.J.: Prentice-Hall, 1969); Perry London, *The Modes and Morals of Psychotherapy* (New York: Holt, 1964).

Chapter 7 Demon Possession

1. C. Fred Dickason, *Angels, Elect and Evil* (Chicago: Moody, 1975), 182.

2. C. Fred Dickason, *Demon Possession and the Christian* (Chicago: Moody, 1987), 89.

3. Ibid., 134.

4. Kurt Koch, *Occult Bondage and Deliverance* (Grand Rapids: Kregel, 1970); also see footnote 5.

5. Based on Dickason, op. cit., 1975, 1987; John P. Newport, "Satan and Demons," in John Warwick Montgomery, ed., *Demon Possession* (Minneapolis: Bethany Fellowship, 1976); Millard J. Sall, "Demon Possession or Psychopathology? A Clinical Differentiation," *Journal of Psychology and Theology*, 1976, 4, pp. 286–90; Samuel Southard, "Demonizing and Mental Illness, Part 2, The Problem of Assessment," *Pastoral Psychology*, 1986, 34, pp. 264–87; Henry C. Virkler and Mary B. Virkler, "Demonic Involvement in Human Life and Illness," *Journal of Psychology and Theology*, 1977, 5, pp. 95–102.

6. Elizabeth Skoglund, *Coping* (Glendale, Calif.: Regal Books, 1979) presents a discussion of Spurgeon's experience of depression.

7. American Psychiatric Association, *Diagnostic and Statistical Manual of Mental Disorders*, Third Edition, Revised (Washington, D.C.: American Psychiatric Association, 1987).

8. See note 5.
9. See 2 Corinthians 11:12–15. For a fascinating description of this process, see Scott Peck, *People of the Lie* (New York: Simon and Schuster, 1983).
10. Dickason, 1987, op. cit., 219.
11. Ibid.; Matt. 17:14–21; Mark 9:7–29; Luke 9:37–43.
12. E.g., see Michael Green, *I Believe in Satan's Downfall* (Grand Rapids: Eerdmans, 1981), especially chapter 3.
13. Dickason, 1975; op. cit., 184.
14. Norman L. Thiessen, *The New Testament Concept of Demonic Possession*, master's thesis, Talbot Theological Seminary, 1975, 10.
15. Ibid., 10–11.

Chapter 8 Demonic Influence and Mental Disorders

1. DSM-III-R uses the term *disorder*, in part to avoid the question of the medical model; see chapter 5.
2. Henry A. Virkler and Mary B. Virkler, "Demonic Involvement in Human Life and Illness," *Journal of Psychology and Theology*, 1977, 5, pp. 95–102.
3. J. Ramsey Michaels, "Jesus and the Unclean Spirits," in John Warwick Montgomery ed., *Demon Possession* (Minneapolis: Bethany Fellowship, 1976).
4. Donald G. Bloesch, *The Reform of the Church* (Grand Rapids: Eerdmans, 1979).
5. See Richard H. Bube, *The Human Quest* (Waco, Tex.: Word, 1971).
6. Millard J. Sall, "Demon Possession or Psychopathology? A Clinical Differentiation," *Journal of Psychology and Theology*, 1976, 4, pp. 286–90; "A Response to 'Demon Possession or Psychopathology? A Theological Relationship,'" *Journal of Psychology and Theology*, 1979, 7, pp. 27–30.
7. Paul J. Bach, "Demon Possession and Psychopathology: A Theological Relationship." *Journal of Psychology and Theology*, 1979, 7, pp. 22–26.
8. American Psychiatric Association, *Diagnostic and Statistical Manual of Mental Disorders*, Third Edition, Revised (Washington, D.C.: American Psychiatric Association, 1980), 29.
9. Ibid., 271.
10. Adapted from Rodger K. Bufford, "The Role of Demonic Factors in Mental Health," presented at the annual convention of the American

Scientific Affiliation, Stanford University, August 1979.

11. Specifically, Narcissistic, Antisocial, and Schizotypal Personality Disorders show some features similar to demon possession; see DSM-III-R, 340–50.

12. DSM-III-R, op. cit.

13. Ibid., 315.

14. Ibid., 255.

15. E.g., C. Fred Dickason, *Demon Possession and the Christian* (Chicago: Moody, 1987).

16. For arguments supporting the view that Christians can be demon possessed, see Ibid., 309; for arguments for a modified or partial possession, see Merrill F. Unger, *What Demons Can Do to Saints* (Chicago: Moody, 1977).

17. Those who believe that Christians cannot be possessed include Grayson H. Ensign and Edward Howe, *Bothered? Bewildered? Bewitched?* (Cincinnati: Recovery, 1984); and Mark I. Bubeck, *The Adversary* (Moody: Chicago, 1975).

18. R. Allison, M.D., and T. Schwarz, *Minds in Many Pieces* (New York: Rawson, Wade, 1980), 196.

19. Ibid., 196.

20. Ibid., 197.

21. Ibid.; it is not clear how Allison and Schwarz propose to distinguish information from the unconscious and that given by a demon.

22. Ibid., 197.

23. Ibid.

24. Ibid., 198.

25. DSM-III-R, op. cit., 340–42.

Chapter 9 Assessment and Diagnosis of Demonic Influence

1. Scott Peck, *People of the Lie* (New York: Simon and Schuster, 1983); see pp. 182–202; Marguerite Shuster, *Power, Pathology and Paradox* (Grand Rapids: Zondervan, 1987), 183–90.

2. C. Fred Dickason, *Demon Possession and the Christian* (Chicago: Moody, 1987), 187.

3. Samuel E. Southard, "Demonizing and Mental Illness, part 2. The Problem of Assessment," *Pastoral Psychology*, 1986, *34*, pp. 264–87.

4. Ibid., 285.

5. Ibid.

6. 1 Cor. 12:8–10; Eph. 4:7–11; Heb. 5:14; 1 John 4:1–6. For a

discussion, see Charles Pfeiffer, Howard Vos, and John Rea, *Wycliffe Bible Encyclopedia,* vol. 1 (Chicago: Moody, 1975), 458.

7. Dickason, op. cit., 330.

8. Albert Runge, "Exorcism: A Satanic Ploy?" *His Dominion,* 1987, *13,* No. 4; pp. 13–18.

9. Ibid., 14.

10. Ibid.; Kurt Koch, *Occult Bondage and Deliverance* (Grand Rapids: Kregel, 1970); Mark I. Bubek, *The Adversary* (Chicago: Moody Press, 1975); Mark I. Bubek, *Overcoming the Adversary* Chicago: Moody Press, 1984).

11. Those with empirical backgrounds will no doubt anticipate correctly that the quality of evidence for this conclusion is weak. It is mostly drawn from case reports and anecdotal data. The strongest support probably comes from Southard, op. cit.

12. See chap. 4.

13. André Kole, a Christian illusionist, draws an important distinction between illusion and magic; magic may lead into demonic influence. For a discussion, see André Kole and Al Janssen, *Miracles or Magic,* revised ed. (Eugene, Ore.: Harvest House, 1987).

14. Southard, op. cit.

15. Robert N. Carson, James N. Butcher, and James C. Coleman, *Abnormal Psychology and Modern Life,* 8th ed. (Glenview, Ill.: Scott-Foresman, 1988). For a more extended discussion, see Sol I. Garfield and Allen E. Bergin, *Handbook of Psychotherapy and Behavior Change,* 3rd ed. (New York: Wiley, 1986).

16. See Donald T. Campbell and Julian C. Stanley, *Experimental and Quasiexperimental Designs for Research* (Boston: Houghton-Mifflin, 1963).

17. Michael Green, *I Believe in Satan's Downfall* (Grand Rapids: Eerdmans, 1981), 133.

18. Ibid., 137.

Chapter 10 Spiritual Interventions

1. See Romans 6:13–23; 1 Cor. 6:18; 10:11–14; 1 Tim. 6:6–11; 2 Tim. 2:20–23; Eph. 5:11–21; 6:10–17; James 5:16; 1 Pet. 5:8–10; 1 John 1:8–9; Rev. 12:11. For a parallel discussion, see Michael Green, *I Believe in Satan's Downfall* (Grand Rapids: Eerdmans, 1981), chapter 8.

2. Rodger K. Bufford, *The Human Reflex: Behavioral Psychology in Biblical Perspective* (San Francisco: Harper and Row, 1981).

3. C. Fred Dickason, *Demon Possession and the Christian* (Chicago: Moody, 1987), 337.

4. Ibid., 343.

5. Lynn Buzzard, *Church Discipline and the Courts* (Wheaton, Ill.: Tyndale House, 1986); J. Carl Laney, *A Guide to Church Discipline* (Minneapolis: Bethany House, 1985); Don Baker, *Beyond Forgiveness: The Healing Touch of Church Discipline* (Portland, Ore.: Multnomah Press, 1984).

6. Lawrence Crabb, Jr., *Basic Principles of Biblical Counseling* (Grand Rapids: Zondervan, 1975), and *Effective Biblical Counseling* (Grand Rapids: Zondervan, 1978).

7. Rodger K. Bufford, "Alternatives to Punishment," *Journal of the American Scientific Affiliation*, 1982, 34, 135–44.

8. Donald R. Peterson, *The Clinical Study of Social Behavior* (Englewood Cliffs, N.J.: Prentice-Hall, 1968); David G. Meyers, *The Human Puzzle* (San Francisco: Harper and Row, 1980).

9. Bert Ghezzi and Mark Kinzer, *Emotions as Resources* (Ann Arbor, Mich.: Servant, 1985).

10. Rodger K. Bufford and Robert E. Buckler, "Counseling in the Church: A Proposed Strategy for Ministering to Mental Health Needs in the Church," *Journal of Psychology and Christianity*, 1987, 6, pp. 21–29.

11. Gordon Borror and Ronald B. Allen, *Worship: Rediscovering the Missing Jewel* (Portland, Ore.: Multnomah Press, 1982).

12. Michael Green, *I Believe in Satan's Downfall* (Grand Rapids: Eerdmans, 1981), 132.

13. Ibid.

14. Dickason proposes several elements in the deliverance of persons from demonization. First, as has already been noted, we must understand biblical teachings about the reality, nature, and activities of demons. Second, understand and rely upon our position and authority in Christ as his servants. Third, prepare for this arduous process by renewing our personal commitment to God, by repudiating false worldviews, and affirming our commitment to God together with the demonized person, forsaking all false ways and their ties—such as occult relics (pictures, amulets, religious relics, ceremonial weapons, and the like), relying on the sixfold armor of God, resisting the forces of evil with commands in the name of Jesus, and responding positively to godly counsel. See Dickason, *Demon Possession* 248–57ff.

15. Ibid., 256–57; also see Marguerite Schuster, *Power, Pathology and Paradox* (Grand Rapids: Zondervan, 1987), 191–94.

16. Dickason, *Demon Possession,* 259.

17. It is Dickason's view that miracles are largely confined to three periods in biblical history: 1) the deliverance of Israel from Egypt; 2) reformation under Elijah and Elisha; 3) introduction of redemption under Christ and the apostles (p. 261). Thus, Dickason does not believe deliverance is miraculous.

Chapter 11 Counseling Approaches

1. American Psychological Association, "Ethical Principles of Psychologists," *American Psychologist,* 1981, *36,* pp. 633–38. After Christ confronted the rich young ruler with what he needed to do in order to enter the kingdom of heaven, the young ruler went away sad (Luke 18:18–27). If Jesus, who knows perfectly what is needful, allows us to choose how we will respond, can we do less for those with whom we counsel?

2. R. Allison and T. Schwarz, *Minds in Many Pieces* (New York: Rawson and Wade, 1980); C. Fred Dickason, *Demon Possession and the Christian* (Chicago: Moody, 1987).

3. See such publications as Claudia Black, *It Will Never Happen to Me* (New York: Ballantine, 1987); Herbert L. Gravitz and Julie D. Bowden, *Guide to Recovery: A Book for Adult Children of Alcoholics* (Holmes Beach, Fla.: Learning Publications, 1985); Sharon Wegscheider-Cruse, *Choicemaking* (Pompano Beach, Fla.: Health Communications, 1985).

4. B. F. Skinner, *Science and Human Behavior* (New York: Free Press, 1953); also see Rodger K. Bufford, *The Human Reflex: Behavioral Psychology in Biblical Perspective* (San Francisco: Harper and Row, 1981).

5. Bufford, "Assertiveness: Recognizing the Limits," *CAPS Bulletin,* 1980, *6* (4), pp. 1–4.

6. Jay Adams helpfully addresses this biblical theme. See Jay E. Adams, *Competent to Counsel* (Grand Rapids: Baker, 1970).

INDEX

Rodger K. Bufford, Ph.D.

Rodger Bufford is chairman of the department of psychology at Western Conservative Baptist Seminary in Portland, Oregon, where he also is on the staff of Western Counseling and Psychological Services Center. Dr. Bufford graduated from The King's College and received his M.A. and Ph.D. from the University of Illinois. He has authored *The Human Reflex: Behavioral Psychology in Biblical Perspective*, as well as numerous articles for professional journals. He and his wife, Kathleen, have two children, Heather and Brett, and make their home in West Linn, Oregon.